EDUCATIONAL STATUS OF RURAL GIRLS

By
KALAWATI

DISCOVERY PUBLISHING HOUSE PVT. LTD.
NEW DELHI-110 002

First Published - 1994

Reprinted - 2013

ISBN: 978-81-7141-239-6

Published by:

DISCOVERY PUBLISHING HOUSE PVT. LTD.
4383/4B, Ansari Road, Darya Ganj
New Delhi-110 002 (India)
Phone: +91-11-23279245; 23253475; 43596065
E-mail: discoverybooksindia@gmail.com
discoverypublishinghouse@gmail.com
web: www.discoverypublishinggroup.com

Printed at:
Infinity Imaging Systems
Delhi

Dedicated
To My
Mother and Mother-in-Law

Preface

One of the most formidable problems which India faces is girls' education. The lack of girls education is the root cause of our growing population, unhygienic living conditions, high death rate and poverty. From my own experience, I have acquired a fair knowledge of the problems in girls' education especially in rural areas. I was interested to write a book about girls' education to highlight some of these problems so that their solution could also be traced.

There has also been a long felt need for a book exclusively on girls' education, in its totality, describing the genesis of various problems and the detailed planning needed to combat each constraint for achieving the objective of enhancing girls' education. I have tried to present various problems in this field and the ways in which these could be solved and girls' education accelerated.

The students and teachers interested in girls' education will surely find this book of some help. This contains first hand information about the problems encountered at home and at school, at personal and at community level. Solutions to these problems and the means to achieve these solutions have also been suggested. The policy makers and the governmental and non-governmental organisations involved in the field of girls' education will also find this book useful. Problems have been illustrated with the help of figures wherever possible. A Model has also been presented which can give a good guidance for planning a programme for girls' education.

I shall be failing in my duty if I do not thank and express my gratitude to the large number of friends who contributed in so many ways to help complete the work. It is impossible to thank commensurately all those who helped. But I must express my special gratitude to Dr. (Mrs.) Parveen Kaur, Dr. R.K. Punia, Dr. (Mrs.) Lali Yadav, Dr. (Mrs.) U. Mehta and Dr. N.P. Singh from CCS Haryana Agriculture University, Hisar who were deeply involved in bringing this work upto this level.

Dr. Kalawati

Acknowledgements

I am highly indebted to my esteemed major adviser, Dr. (Mrs.) Parveen Kaur, Associate Professor, Department of Child Development, College of Home Science, CCS Haryana Agricultural University, Hisar, for her precious guidance, intellectual stimulation, continuing and sustained encouragement, untiring help and her unflinching interest with great love and affection throughout the present study.

I express my deep sense of gratitude and sincere thanks to Dr. (Miss) M. Nath, former Head of the Department of Child Development, for her initial guidance and keen interest in the present study. Grateful acknowledgements are also due to the members of my advisory committee, Dr. R.K. Punia, Dr. (Mrs.) Lali Yadav, Dr. (Mrs.) Usha Mehta, Dr. (Mrs.) S. Chhikara, Dr. L.S. Kaushik and Dr. A.C. Kapoor for their valuable suggestions, great interest and constructive criticism during the course of study.

Thanks are also due to the faculty members of Department of Child Development for their valuable help and kind cooperation in the present study.

I am also thankful to Dr. N.P. Singh, former Assistant Professor, Department of Mathematics and Statistics, for the computer analysis of the data.

I wish to express my sincere thanks to the Headmasters/Headmistresses of all the selected schools and the respondents of this study for their cooperation in data collection. The present study would have remained unfinished without their active involvement.

I am thankful to Shri Subhash Chandra for taking hard pains in typing the manuscript nicely and to Shri Kuljit Mann for his appreciable efforts in preparing graphs.

I am thankful to my husband Er. R.S. Malik for his inspiration and help at right moments. He gave valuable suggestions for the study and kept my morale high whenever I lost courage. I am indebted to my daughter Arunima who was deprived of her due share of time from her mother due to the present study. She, inspite of her tender age behaved well and provided comic relief at appropriate and occasionally inappropriate times.

I owe my gratitude to my respected father-in-law for his good wishes, encouragement, inspiration and help throughout my Ph.D. programme. My sincere thanks are due to my mother-in-law, sisters-in-law for their best wishes and the extra burden of household jobs which they had to share during my busy days.

I am thankful to my mother, sister and the younger brother who remained concerned about the progress of the present study.

I am thankful to my brothers-in-law, Dr. F.S. Nandal and Mr. Arvind Singh, for their help and support.

The financial help provided by UNDP in the shape of Senior Fellowship is fully acknowledged.

Finally, I am thankful to all those who have helped me directly or indirectly in completing the present study.

Kalawati

Contents

Preface

Acknowledgements

1. Introduction **1**

2. Review of literature **10**

Familial factors and scholastic achievement
School and community related factors
Psychological characteristics

3. Methodology **29**

4. Results and Discussion **44**

Scholastic achievements of high school girl students
Perceived constraints and attitude
General information about the teachers
Scholastic achievements of girl students in relation to socio-personal, economic and psychological characteristics
Strategy for enhancing the scholastic achievements of girl students.

5. Summary and conclusion **146**

Bibliography 152

Index 167

1

Introduction

"Educated men are as much superior to Uneducated as the living are to the dead".

—Aristotle

Education is the deliberate and systematic influence, exerted by a mature person upon the immature, through instruction or supporting the harmonious development of physical, intellectual, aesthetic, social and other abilities of human beings by providing appropriate stimulation and environment. Etymologically, the term 'education' comes from the Latin word 'educare' which means 'bringing up' or 'to nourish'. It indicates that education is a process of training the individual through various experiences of life so as to draw out the best in him.

According to Dewey (1916) education is the process through a continuous reconstruction of experiences. It is the development of all those capacities in the individual which enable him to control his environment and fulfil his responsibilities in more effective manner. In a broader sense 'education' is for bringing-up of the young child in best of the way the child is capable of and in the way the society needs it. The education must also encompass the acquisition of good habits, values and attitudes.

The cultural development of any nation largely depends upon the educational system. Any society without education is not a society but rowdy, uncouth and unfeeling crowd of childish men and women. An educated society would manifest itself in the qualities of tolerance, progress, harmony and fellow feeling. It is through education that every generation transmits to the next, its social heritage. Like social transformation, the economic development also rests upon education. Thus, it is like a catalyst in the process of social and cultural development. It is not out of place to say that our greatest sin is the neglect of the masses and that is the cause of our downfall.

Our Prime Minister Shri P.V. Narasimha Rao rightly stressed that it is for the national development or integration; social cohesion or cultural advancement or preservation of democracy that we should achieve a hundred per cent literacy among our people.

Men, women and children all should be educated, it will be of greater value if right foundation is laid right from the beginning. The fact that children form the foundation of a strong and healthy nation has been universally recognised and emphasised again and again. It is through proper education that a child can be helped to develop his skill, ability, character and personality who then shows new lights of hope to the younger generation.

Some may find the experiences of life as the best teacher. This may be true in certain restricted spheres. The experiences of life may help in learning but shooling has its own role in helping child unfold his potentialities. To prepare a child to control his environment and native impulses and also to reorganise and restructure his experiences, schooling is essential. Thus, the strongest force in development and growth of a child for preparing him to be responsible, innovative, socially and culturally well-adjusted is the school education.

The educational status in society has rested upon social, political and economic conditions. The historic perspective of educational development may be helpful in viewing the problem in proper perspectives. The history of development of education in Haryana, may be divided in four sub periods; the first, from 1800-1857 (under the East India Company's Rule), the second, from 1858 to 1900 (under the Crown) and the third from 1901 to 1947 (under the Crown, in the age of national awakening) and the fourth 1948-1991 (after independence). Under the East India Company's rule, in Haryana, peasants were in a great majority and considered education as useless and hence never sent their children to school. As a result there were no schools in rural Haryana.

A brief account of the early 19th century reveals that in the lower region i.e. in the districts of Rohtak, Hisar and Gurgaon there were 27 muslim schools with 886 pupils and 70 teachers. In the upper region, i.e. in the districts of Karnal, etc. the position was equally bad. In Sonepat, there were only 3 schools. In the town of Panipat there were several ill supported and thinly attended schools. In the town of Karnal with 20,000 population there was only one school. Elsewhere in 18 mosque schools there were 227 pupils. The courses of taching in these schools were very elementary in type and there were no formal examinations and pupils were promoted to the next higher class as and when found fit by the teacher (Shankar and Kundu, 1970).

In the beginning of 19th century, government and some individuals in the service of the East India Company made some positive gesture to spread education. In Haryana such an individual was Fraser. Unaided by any government or private agency this officer established four schools from 1816 to 1823. Later, another energetic person the Lieutenant Governor of the Province, James Thomson, proposed to establish schools in every village of a certain size (of about 200 houses). This led to the establishment of government middle schools one in each Tehsildari. Subsequently besides many schools, a few high schools were also established at Karnal, Rohtak, Bhiwani, Rewari, Delhi and Jagadhari. Schools mostly began to cater to the needs of peasantry and subjects taught were closely connected with agricultural pursuits and requirements. Ambala district was the most benefitted. It had one school for every ten square miles. Karnal and Gurgaon had one for every fifteen square miles and Rohtak had eighteen. Hisar was the most backward district in this regard. It had one school for forty nine square miles. Thus, the extent of educational benefits remained meagre. A large number of children who ought to have gone to schools remained at home and received no education at all. Infact, the villagers had no interest in education as it was of little use for them in their daily life. Moreover, it had many barriers also. Only enlightened and rich people in the cities took a lead in this direction in the early part of 19th century (Herold, 1971).

Girls' education, despite of the efforts of the government could not be popularized in this region. By the end of 19th century there was no middle or high school for them and only primary schools were there. This shows that the position of education in Haryana region was far from satisfactory. A bulk of the population remained uneducated due to various cultural and historical reasons. However, an era of awakening began with the Punjab Primary Act, 1919 which led to an increase in the number of primary, middle and high schools. Many schools for girls were also started. But as regards quality of education and peoples participation, the response remained poor. Hence, the percentage of literacy remained very low. The quality of education was also substandard (Indira and Sujatha, 1988).

After independence the number of schools started increasing. Now almost every village has a school. In some of the villages of Haryana there are separate schools for girls upto primary or middle level. But, in Hisar district very few villages have separate girl schools. As per policy, girls and boys both have equal right of getting school education. Girls today stand a better chance of going to school than their mothers did. Yet, even today women constitute the larger proportion of illiterates. About 75 per cent of the adult illiterates in India are women (Census, 1991). No nation can progress if the women were left behind, as they constitute fifty per cent of work force and also they make the healthy future force of the nation. In fact, she is the bigger strength of man-force also. Thus, ignoring women means stagnating all social, economical and political advancements.

Shri Morarji Desai, our the then Prime Minister while inaugurating a three day National Conference on "Women and Development" organised by the Development Bureau of the Department of Social Welfare in 1979 expressed, "If women are literate then there will be no illiterate children in the country". Mahatma Gandhi also strongly advocated the women's education. In his words, "When you educate a man, you educate an individual but when you educate a women, you educate a family".

Literacy is one aspect, another aspect is higher and advanced education. It is, although important that women be made aware of their aspirations, their real potentials and their rights, if society wants to eliminate the sex discriminations. This would result into the promotion of women's participation in political, economic and cultural fields.

According to Puri (1991) four to six years of mothers' schooling reduces deaths of children in their first 12 months by as much as 20 per cent. Every additional year of education results in a drop upto 9 per cent in deaths of children upto the age of six. A one per cent rise in women literacy maybe three times more effective in reducing child mortality than one per cent rise in the number of doctors. The level of education of mother also seems to affect the quality of life indicators such as infant mortality rate, birth rate, sex ratio and the percentage of married females in the age group of 15-19 years.

The intellectual level of mother has also been found to influence the expression of genetic predisposition for mental retardation in children. In homes in which the father is of average intelligence but the mother is retarded, retardation is two and a half times more frequent among the children than in homes with equally retarded fathers and normal I.Q. mothers (Reed and Reed, 1965). But unfortunately the society itself is eliminating the women. The declining sex ratio, from 972 females per 1000 males in 1901 to 929 females per 1000 males in 1991 reflects the degraded value for a girl child. For Haryana, the sex ratio is further alarming. During the year 1901 there were 867 females per 1000 males and during the year 1991, there are 874 females per 1000 males. Though, the number of females per thousand males have marginally increased yet the sex ratio of females is very low. A significant demographic imbalance indicates towards the degraded position of girls which is also supported by census report for Indian female literacy which is pegged only at 39.42 as compared to 63.86 for males (Census, 1991).

Mothers are the prime source of proper physical, mental and moral development of their children. A child begins to know his environment, learns his food habits, social manners, skills, values and attitudes from his mother. Hence, it is important for the mother herself to have the right kind of education. An educated mother can perform her role more efficiently.

Besides founding the proper schooling of girls, it is although more important to see that they perform well and also that they continue to study further. This aspect is related to the Psyche' of the girls which again depends upon what way parents, teachers and community have created impressions upon them. Going to school or registration in schools would not mean anything by itself. Success depends upon the performance which can be measured through the tests. This achievement in the school or college may be taken to mean any desirable learning that has been acquired by students. Since the word 'desirable' implies a value judgement, it is obvious that a particular learning may be referred to as achievement. This way any behaviour that is learned may come within the scope of achievement. Though, the spectrum of learning is not limited to mere acquisition of information, it also includes attitudes, interests, values, etc. However, schools and colleges are concerned to a great extent with the development of knowledge, understanding and acquisition of skills. In other words, the 'learning' which educational institutions concern themselves, is predominantly intellectual. Pressey Robysen and Herroch (1941) define achievement as "it is a status or level of learning and his ability to apply what he has learnt".

Academic achievement is related to the acquisition of principles and generalizations and the capacity to perform efficiently certain manipulations of objects, symbols and ideas. Assessment of academic performance has been largely confined to the evaluation in terms of examination. The performance of the student in those examinations is the academic performance termed as the scholastic achievement of the student.

Trow (1956] defines academic achievement as "the attained ability or degree of competence in school tasks." Good (1959) refers to academic achievement as "the knowledge attained or skill developed in the school subjects is usually designated by test scores or marks assigned by teachers", Academic achievements assume primary importance in the context of an education system aimed at progressive scholastic development of the child and human resources development at the macro-level. The further education of a child depends upon the nature of his academic success. Another analysis reveals that the academic development is uniform, regular and steady and is shown through the gradual progress in achievement from year to year. Achievement encompasses enhancement of "self actualisation" or as Maslow would say, "self improvement" and some forms of competitiveness. Successes act as emotional tonic.

Scholastic success serves as the foundation for further studies as well as a source of inspiration for higher achievements. One success leads to another. Better foundation results in sound physical, social and psychological development of the child. Thus, scholastic achievement is one of the most important pre-requisite which stimulates the individual to perform specialized roles with different degress of allotted prestige and rewards. Scholastic achievement in case of girls is much important because their further studies depend largely upon the level of their achievements. If boy fails, parents would bear it and give other chances but if girl fails, they will not allow her to continue. If she is an excellent performer, she may have chances of continuing education further.

There are number of factors that affect the scholastic achievement. The subjective factors affecting scholastic achievement are individualistic in nature and would include intelligence, learning ability, aptitude, self concept, perception of school, study method, motivation, anxiety, interests, social and emotional adjustment, aspirations, etc. Some of the objective factors which influence the child in his level of achievement are his socio-economic status, educational facilities, examination system, personality of the teacher, psychological environment at home and family relations of the child.

There are many barriers in the education of girls which affect their achievements. As the early childhood get over, a young girl starts helping her parents in the household chores. Yet, she is considered to be "Paraya Dhan" (Others' property) and investment in her is difficult to justify. Her marriage is a drain on the family's resources. Moreover, there is a common belief that educated women will not adjust in her in-laws family. Thus, her education would not only be a total wastage but hinderance in marriage also. An educated women demands autonomy hence, may not surrender to others. The pushing forces may compel her to leave school regardless of her scholastic success or progress. Parental apathy towards girls' education is the main root cause behind her educational backwardness. Studies have shown that parental practices that engender emotional security and low anxiety, independence and high internalized goals for achievement are associated with accelerated cognitive development in children. Parents who value achievement and set high achievement standards may have children who have high achievement motivation and make more sustained efforts to attain their goals. Although parental behaviours are related to achievement in children; other factors such as, social class, education and social opportunities set important limits on the attainments of children. Due to such barriers in the women's education the performance level of girls in schools go on decreasing.

It is important to find out the root cause of low achievement, in this region also. Therefore, to suggest remedial measures to reduce, if not eliminate this problem, the present study was undertaken with the following objectives.

Objectives

1. To find out the scholastic achievements of the rural high school girls.
2. To assess the factors affecting scholastic achievements of the girl students.
3. To suggest a strategy for enhancing the scholastic achievements of the girls.

Limitations of the Study

The study has obvious limitation of area, time, and other resources as faced by a single student researcher. Secondly, the study was conducted in the selected villages of Hisar district, which may limit the generalization of findings to other areas.

Scope of the Study

The findings of the present study may provide a guideline to the government and non government agencies for further analysis of the problem. The identified problems and strategy planned for the solution of the problems would help the extention workers and researchers to make this as a base for starting some intervension programmes in the villages.

The solution of the identified problems can strengthen the school programme and also can give guidelines for other agencies involved in education of girls. It is expected that interaction of various institutions or systems involved in teaching-learning situation of girls can prove to be practical significance.

The solution of the problems based on the perception of rural girls, their parent and the teachers will add to pragmatic approach to the girl students, their parents and teachers. In context to the national problems, the different solutions of the problems can help in strengthening the programmes on the desired lines.

2

Review of Literature

This chapter deals with the review of literature which have direct or indirect relevance to the problem under investigation. The attempts have been made to record the available literature under following sections :

- Familial factors and scholastic achievement
  - Family background
  - Home constraints
  - Attitude and values of parents
- School and community related factors and scholastic achievement
  - School factors
  - Community factors
- Other psychological characteristics and scholastic achievement
  - Achievement motivation
  - Academic anxiety
  - Level of aspiration

Familial Factors and Scholastic Achievement

Family background. The studies related to the impact of family's socio-economic and other factors date back to as old as four decades. Abrahasan (1952) found achievement closely related to social class position and there are large number of studies in subsequent years. However, there are many studies which support the findings of Abrahasan (1952) and many do not. The latter studies cover the wider range of variables that affect school achievement of children. Hence, in this chapter an effort is being made to accommodate the studies mainly conducted in last two decades and omitting others conducted before that period. However, a few important studies of 1960's are also being described. Six years after Abrahasan's study Stephans (1958) reported economic factors having very little to do with the performance of the child in the school. Out of the various family factors, the education of the parents showed the closest relation and income the least but positive relation with the school performance of the children.

Kaur (1961) during her study on 600 students conducted in Patiala found a highly significant correlation in the income of parents and the scholastic achievements of their children. Whereas, Singh (1962) found a very low correlation between economic status of the parents and the achievement of the children in schools. He also observed that the educational status of the parents is not a factor of primary importance in determining the academic performance of the children.

Medsker (1963) concluded that the fathers' occupation, parents' education and the family encouragement were influencial to the attendance as well as performance of the children in the examination.

Chopra (1964) keeping the effect of intelligence constant obtained the socio-economic factors as affecting academic achievement. He found that 96 per cent drop outs leave the school because of poor economic conditions of the family. Students belonging to the higher qualitative group on the basis of parents' education, occupation, family income, and cultural level of the family showed significantly higher achievement.

Deutsch (1964) obtained father's presence in homes as an important factor. Fatherless children have obtained significantly lower intelligence test scores. By the time they reached the fifth grade there was lack of interaction between the parents and the child. This reduced interaction initiated less intellectual stimulation of the child.

Elder (1965) studied the educational attainment in relation to family structure and found that the size of family, birth place, religion and the social class were associated with the educational achievement. Parental dominance retained its effect even when these variables were controlled.

Mehta (1966) found that boys having low educated fathers and having fathers doing some kind of skilled or unskilled work showed higher achievement than those who had petty shops.

Plowden (1967) reported that not only the physical amenities of the home but number of dependent children, father's occupational group and parents' education also affected the educational achievement of the child in the school. He also found that more variation in children's school achievement is specially accounted for by the variation in parental attitudes than by either the variation in material circumstances of the parents or by the variation in the school. The relative importance of the parental attitude increase as the children grew older.

Chopra (1969) while studying the boys of secondary schools in Lucknow found that marks obtained by high socio-economic group in all subjects were significantly higher than those obtained by the other socio-economic groups. There was positive relationship between socio-economic background and achievement in English, Mathematics and Science but no relationship between socio-economic background and marks in Hindi, Biology and Art.

Singh (1969) conducted a study on 85 student-teachers, to find out the students' educational problems with regard to their fathers' occupation. The study revealed that 70 per cent of the fathers of children with educational problem were engaged in independent occupations, like business, agriculture, medicine and cloth-washing. They were busy throughout the day and did not find time to look after their children. Thirty per cent of fathers were either clerks, teachers, officers or employees in a factory/mill. The nature of the work of the first group demanded more time and energy so as to curb their interaction with their children. Whereas, the achievement was high in the second group of respondents.

Mathur and Hundal (1972) employed a correlational technique to establish relationship between school achievement, intelligence and some socio-economic background factors. A relationship between achievement and socio-economic background factors was obtained. It was also noticed that the larger the family, the lower the achievement and intelligence of the child when the other factors were kept constant. Parents' education and income were found to have direct influence on the achievement of the child.

Sinha (1973) also found father's occupation as significantly associated with students' scholastic achievement whereas the social class did not bear any relevance in this regard.

Dhami (1974) conducted a survey on 586 high school students of both the sexes from 60 schools of Punjab and found the relationship between the socio-economic status and the scholastic achievement which was statistically significant but not very high. This shows that whatever is the socio-economic position of a learner, his achievement is better related to other factors.

Ahluwalia and Shyam (1975), Saini (1977) and Ganpathy and Singh (1981) also found very little to negligible impact of SES on academic achievement. Whereas Srivastava *et. al.* (1975) and Kundu (1977) found socio-economic conditions of the family significantly affecting the academic performance of children.

Rajguru *et. al.* (1975) concluded that the students having fathers or guardian parents educated upto the primary school standard, having three or more educated persons in the family though belonging to lower socio-economic group had a higher percentage of success over others.

Ports and Wilson (1976) studied the black-white differences in educational attainment on the basis of a longitudinal sample of the U.S high school population. Black led higher educational attainment than Whites of similar parental status and ability. Differences in process of educational attainment pointed to the stronger relative role of parental status, measured ability and school grades among Whites and of self esteem and educational aspirations among Blacks.

Zajone (1976) found that the brightest children generally are those born early in the smallest families, perhaps because they get a good deal of undivided adult attention in their early years. Birth spacing also appeared to make a difference as longer spacing between children made it possible to give each child more attention during the early years of life.

Mani (1980) reported that a large percentage of drop outs (52%) belonged to the larger families (with five or more members). Since child had to adjust and live with a number of other siblings, the problem of maladjustment and jealousy might have led to the problem of drop outs. Parental illiteracy and poverty compelled their children to be out of school and being at home they provided additional hand to parents

Sharma (1982) also reported parental education as highly associated with the academic achievement of their sons and daughters.

Siddique *et al.* (1983) while studying the factors affecting academic achievement of school children found socio-economic conditions of the family affecting academic performance. However, various psycho-social factors were also found important behind academic performance.

Contractor (1984) observed some background factors *viz.*, birth order, mothers' education, number of siblings and size of household as affecting scholastic performance of students. The investigation showed that high achievers had higher mother's education level, less number of siblings, restricted size of household and more number of rooms in the residence than that of low achievers.

Mittal and Nand (1984) found that as high as 79 per cent of students who showed low performance belonged to the families with agriculture as their main occupation. Another 10 per cent had labour as their main occupation. The poor educational background, joint or large family size, small land holding, parents' indifference attitude towards education, child's assistance in farm or family work, financial strain, children's lack of interest in studies and non-professional nature of education were found affecting child's school performance.

Jagannathan (1986) found that children hailing from the families which subscribe to newspapers and magazines progress better than their educational attainments, which might be due to their constant contact with the rich literature they were provided with.

Kharb (1990) studied the school achievement of rural and urban children in age group of 10-12 years and found that socio-economic status has a positive and marked to very high relationship with school achievement.

To sum up, it can be said that some of the studies hold socio-economic status and social class position as responsible for the low and high achievement of the children. In other studies, socio-economic stuatus and social class position does not bear any effect on scholastic achievements of children. A substantial number of studies supported parents' education, occupation, family income, number of children and the size of family as reponsible for performance of children in school. Birth spacing and birth order were also found responsible for the scholastic achievement of children.

Home Constraints. Home environment and other family characteristics constitute one of the most important factors that determine the level of achievement of child in the school.

Rosen and D'Andrade (1959) demonstrated that boys having dominant mothers or mothers with lesser expectation of self reliance in their children had high achievement than the others. Though, such mothers had higher aspirations for their sons and greater concern over their success.

Ojha (1966) obtained that parents, put their children in schools when they are six years old and not of much use in household work or as a aid to the field work. Parents withdraw them at the age of nine when they can fully participate in rendering assistane to their parents in various ways.

Venkata Subramanian and Kulandaivel (1968) found that significantly higher percentage of girls than boys reported illness, and work at home as the cause of absence from school. Significantly more percentage of boys than girls reported helping parents and shopping for home as the cause of their absence from school.

Chopra (1970) studied 640 students of the class X randomly selected from six urban and two rural higher secondary schools in Lucknow and found that 68 per cent of the educated fathers supervised students' studies at home and helped them in their studies. Apart from this they had comparatively better cultural atmosphere. In their homes they had more books and subscribed magazines and newspapers. Students from homes with good cultural atmosphere got higher scores and marks than the students from less educated families.

Joseph (1973) while investigating the relationship between educational environment in the home and student achievement obtained a correlation of 0.756 ($P<0.01$) on a sample of grade 5, controlling for intelligence the correlation was 0.648($P<0.01$). For grade 7, the r was 0.783 ($P<0.01$), with intelligence controlled, the correlation was 0.617 ($P<0.01$).

Ismail (1975) investigating on the causes of girl drop outs observed that the school work was hard to combine with household chores and opined that whenever young girls found some time for their studies, they were called away by their mothers to attend to some domestic work. At a time when boys were busy between school books and play in rural countryside, their sisters were already immersed in the drudgery of domestic chores.

Dalela (1976) reported that in punjab only 8 per cent of the total time of girls belonging to farm labourers was spent in schools.

Jackson and Marsden (1976) advocated social-cultural factors as important in achievement of middle class children who were facilitated by books, liberal speech patterns at home disigned so as to help child's vocabulary, more opportunity for travel and stimulation through educational visits, higher level of parental expectation, economic provision to stay at school after the age of sixteen and home work facilities and even private tutors.

Sen Gupta (1976) reported that because of poverty artisan could not afford to educate his wards despite free of cost education. In fact for him uneducated child was an asset whereas education becomes liability because of loss of earnings made by the child. Many of such non-school going kids or drop outs migrate to cities to beg or to find work to earn money.

Khanna (1977) reported that the girls dropped out of school because of parents' negative attitude towards education especially for girls. They were to get married and move to another house for which education served no specific purpose. The other reasons given by the author were extra hand needed at home, the faulty environment in the school and the unrealistic school curriculum.

Aggarwal (1978) studied 171 tenth class girls of three government schools in Chandigarh and found though the average score on family relations of low achievers was higher than that of average score of high achievers, the co-efficient of correlation between academic achievement and family relations was 0.31 which shows that these two variables are correlated but extent of correlation is low.

Dhar (1978) opined that since some students had to

assist in augmenting the income of the households, they cannot attend schools when the normally function. He further observed that the bulk of the drop outs took place when the child was just beginning his schooling between class I and II, he was too young to be of any great economic use to the household which he attributedt o the school environment like inadequately trained teachers, dull and ill-equipped schools and irrelevant curriculum.

Bhargava (1979) reported that children from weaker rural sections of society did not attend the school because education could not satisfy the demands of their life. As a result from every 100 children admitted in class I oniy 40 could reach upto class V and 25 upto middle.

Muralidharan (1980) reported that most important reason for no-enrolment and low achievement of the rural children was the chronic proverty of the rural population, as result of which children were engaged in occupations to supplement their family income. These findings were later supported by Sudha and Tiwari (1985).

Saroj Bala (1980) obtained poor level of scholastic achievement in rural Haryana as 11.66 per cent students secured first division and 37.78 per cent second division. The remaining half of the students feel in the category of third division or failure. The scholastic achievement of the female students was poor because of traditional and conservative mental make up of the parents. Other related factors were lack of time due to assisting in family occupation, family size, educational environment of the family, place to study, interest of teachers in the studies, self interest of students and parental income.

Bhaskaran (1989) found that daily shopping for all family, looking after younger children and running the home are often the responsibility of girls aged ten and over, especially, in economically disadvantaged households. The tendency to make use of the labour of girls in the household is astonishingly acute, resulting in girls being forced to leave school, regardless of their scholastic success or progress.

The available studies show that parental behaviour and family relations and educational environment at home are important for the school performance of the children. In most of the studies, it was lack of time which affected the performance of the students. Children getting more books, subscribed magazines and newspapers alongwith better home work facilities and private tutors had better performance than the others.

Attitude and values of parents. Crandall *et al.* (1964) did not find any relation between the parental encouragement and participation in intellectual activities with their child and the school performance of these children. Further, no relation between the value of fathers and mothers placed upon their children's intellectual performance was observed.

Rai (1971) reported that many parents were reluctant to sent their daughters to schools because of the present of male teachers and lack of separate school for girls.

Ulldriks (1972) studied 50 individual cases from two working class neighbourhoods in Holland and found that the family value factors are of greater significance in educational achievement than either family status or famil y structure.

Mehra (1977) reported that women's education was adversely affected by parental attitude besides many other socio-cultural factors.

Mehta (1977) found the traditional customs as important behind rural girls' unsatisfactory education. Such, traditional customs forbid the girls' school going.

Bose (1978) while studying the parental attitude and academic achievement found that mothers of high achiever and low achiever groups differ significantly.

Sinha (1983) revealed that in higher income and education groups higher was the number of women having favourable attitude towards education of women.

Shah and Nagia (1984) found that majority of rural mothers had favourable attitude towards the primary education of their daughters. The favourable attitudes were found more amongst the respondents who belonged to the village having good educational facilities, who were literate and belonged to high and middle socio-economic group.

Saraswathi and Radhika (1985) conducted a study to examine the attitudes of rural women of the scheduled castes and tribes in Gujarat state, towards the value of education. Seven of the 30 women interviewed expressed that education offered no gain especially through daughters. Women ultimately have to do domestic work only. Some of the women opined that education did more harm than good, especially in the case of girls because educated girls fail to acquire skills in farming and household work and get out of hand with changed attitudes and behaviour. Education according to them was more important for boys than for girls as boys earn and support parents in old age. Education was found irrelavant for the kind of life girls had to subsequently lead. Educated girls demand autonomy.

Charyulu (1987) observed that education of women was considered as important all by women in general though more by upper caste and less by middle caste. Women considered Balwadi, or pre-schools as important beginning. Fifty per cent opined in favour of girls' education as it helps in getting better bride grooms, however, the cost of marriage increases. The opinion against sending girls for education or employment outside still persisted because of the fear of their being immoral or polluted.

Singh (1988) obtained a close relationship between socio-cultural handicaps and basic family attitudes and parental behaviour like rigidity, permissiveness, authority, comprehension, dialogue, etc., as closely related to child's performance in school.

It is evident from the studies that attitude of the parents towards the education of their children and the values possessed by the family members are the important factors which determine the achievement of the children in school.

School and Community Related Factors

School factors. Rai (1975) reported that the causes

of low education in rural areas were dearth of women teachers, more mature school girls in villages and co-education schools. The enrolment of girls was poor and drop out rate high. In primary stage of education one girl out of three is dropped. Only 80 per cent reach up to class VIII from class VI.

Daniel (1976) observed that a significant majority of children going for child labour were either school drop outs or those who had never gone to school. Economic factors forced children to work as child labour. School education did not satisfy the psycho-economic and social needs of the child nor was it well-designed to deal with the individual differences.

Gupta (1976) reported influence of the school and its environment, attitude of the parents and demand they make on time and abilities of children and change of residence as a reason for a wastage and stagnation in the elementary school education in the country.

Kitchen (1976) reported that attendance in the school, grade point average and other school activities showed a moderately low but significant positive relationship with parental characteristics of ethnic origin.

Shukla (1983) found the student population of high performance secondary school as superior in intelligence and SES. The physical facilities were distinctly better in high performance schools. High performance schools were distinctly superior to low performance schools both in curricular and co-curricular activities.

Saleh (1985) assessed the relative effect of classroom, schooling and background factors on students' progress in schools. He found that students' prior preparation, educational experience, teachers, quality and classroom climate had direct, positive and significant effect on academic achievement while parents' SES and school organizational complexity had little effect.

Saraswathi and Radhika (1985) highlighted that the education offered in schools today has little in common with the existing pattern of socialization of girls in a rural setting. The girls are drilled to listen and not to speak before elders; neither to express their opinion nor to oppose elders decisions. The perceived irrelevance of education was viewed as a major constraint in progress of education of girls.

White (1987) conducted a ex-post facto study on 39 teachers and 819 students in grades seven, nine and eleven located in a single south-west Florida school district. It was found that the student achievement was related with school climate as well as classroom climate.

Routray (1988) studied the effect of teacher's involvement in scholastic achievement of 300 pupils of eighth, ninth and tenth class from six secondary schools of Cuttak district in Orissa. He found that as regards the average students, teacher's involvement and attiude are found to have positive and significant relationship with the academic achievement.

Skiera (1990) holds the defective system of teaching responsible for poor performance of children in school. Subjects taught were insufficiently related to the fundamental interests of the child.

Shah (1991) while exploring the factors associated with the low enrolment of girls in schools as obtained less number of female teachers, large number of single teacher schools, lower enrolment of girls and high drop out rates resulting in the lower percentage of girls appearing for matriculation examination. Only 27 per cent of the students who appeared for the examination in 1983-84 were girls.

The studies on school related factors show that the lack of teachers, teacher's quality, classroom climate and school performance of the students. The other factors related to school are physical facilities in the school and defective system of teaching which are also related to the performance of the students.

Community related factors

Jorapur (1972) after conducting studies in Malnad areas of Karnatka, revealed that literacy and educational level was associated with the rate of early marriages.

Ahuja (1973) opined that the social, economic and political factors like rural customs and traditions were opposing girls' education. More importance was given to boys educations of the parents, lack of schooling facilities, early marriage, lack of good women leadership to promote women's education. The attitude of women towards girls' education was also significant.

Kashyap (1974) reported the growth of female literacy is markedly low in rural areas because of the social circumstances like the social discriminations between sexes and girls' early marriages, Much involvement in field work and household work also hindered the girls' education.

Pillai (1975) reported that a large number of women in India were illiterate because of apprehension that educated women could not participate in economic programmes due to the traditional view point that women's role is to be wife, mother and home maker only. Moreover, the social pressures confined women to the lower status. Thirdly, the inadequate educational system itself put her out of school. Shamsuddin (1975) also found low participation of girls due to child marriage, indifference of parents towards education of their daughters, lack of faith in the system of girl's education and economic pressure on middle class people, etc.

Bhandari (1982) also reported that the main reasons for non-attendance and low performance of girls were negative opinion of the village community towards girl's education, cultural constraints and traditions and strong opposition to co-educational system.

Talesra (1986) while interviewing 500 girl students of college in Udaipur, Rajasthan found in rural areas there were lesser facilities provided for women to receive higher education. The notion of virginity and chastity associated with the sacred character of marriage and apprehension regarding their being polluted were in the way of women's coming for higher education. The practice of child marriage, dowry and purdah had their base in the institutional structure of the society. There existed some primordial traditional and belief structures which came in the way of higher education.

From the above cited studies, it emerged out that the major community factors affecting girls' education are early marriage, dowry and purdah system in village community. Discrimination among boys and girls is another factor affecting girls' education.

Psychological Characteristics

Achievement motivation. Lakshmi (1967) tried a new theme and experimentally established relationship between the rate of learning and achievement motive in high school boys. She showed that fast learners had higher achievement motivation than slow learners.

Mehta (1969) obtained low positive correlation between mark in various school subjects and need achievement in the annual examination.

Raynor (1970) reported that students received higher grades in a particular college course were high in need achievement and low in test anxiety.

Gokulnathan (1971) did not find achievement motivation bearing significant relationship to academic achievement of both boys and girls.

Bhangoo and Lakshmi (1975) while studying achievement motivation among rural and urban boys found that school achievement was significantly and positively correlated with achievement motivation of the urban boys group but not significant in rural boys group.

Kirpal Kaur (1976) found that there existed a positive and significant relationship between achievement motivation and academic achievement in mathematics when tested on 200 nienth grade students of both the sexes taken from the Model Schools of Chandigarh in the age group of about thirteen years. She also found a significant negative correlation between anxiety and academic achievement among these students.

Vora (1977) showed that reading comprehension and need-achievement have positive relationship.

Parikh (1978) while studying the seconday school pupils of VIII, IX and X standards in Bombay obtained that school performance is positively and highly related to achievement motivation.

Christian (1980) in a study with 500 girl students of Sardar Patel University from pre-university to postgraduate classes in all streams; Arts, Science, Commerce, Engineering, Home Science and Education found that mean scores of those who obtained 1st division or who failed, on need-achievement were more or less the same and that of third divisioners was highest. Hence, there was no relationship between achievement motivation and academic performance. Anxiety did not show any effect on performance.

Usha Kharangar (1983) did not find need for achievement as significantly correlated with total performance at the school annual examination.

Tandani (1984) while studying the relationship between achievement motivation and academic achievement on a sample of 101 socially-deprived students of Xth class, found achievement motivation as significantly influencing academic achievement.

Rajput (1984) could not find the achievement of students in mathematics as affected by their achievement motivation under the neutral classroom conditions. Whereas, Sween (1984) found the two groups – high need-achievement and low on need-achievement groups differing in their gain scores on the criterion test. High achievement motivated students gained significantly more than those with low achievement motivation.

Kingra (1986) administered Rao's achievement motivation test on ninth class students selected randomly from six rural schools of Ludhiana district and found a significant negative correlation between achievement motivation and academic achievement. The same was supported by Kaur (1988) while conducting a study on 350 students of both sexes studying in IX class in English medium schools of Chandigarh city.

Mehar (1991) conducted a study on a sample of 100 students both boys and girls randomly selected from different high schools of rural and urban areas of Karnal district. No significant correlation between the achievement motivation and academic achievement was found. However, Singh (1991) using Rao's Achievement Motivation Test found achievement motivation as positively correlated with academic achievement.

Thus, some of the studies have shown the relationship between achievement motivation and academic performance of the students while others did not.

Academic Anxiety

Atkinson and Litwin (1960) and Bartlett and Smith (1966) found an insignificant negative relationship between academic achievement and anxiety. Same was found long back by Sarason and Madler (1952).

Cauble (1965) found (i) high anxious children as less capable at complex tasks than low moderate anxious children, (ii) high anxious children with a tendency to have lower intelligence quotient, (iii) high anxious children with high intelligence were no more able to perform complex tasks than high anxious children with more 'normal' intelligence and (iv) high anxiety associated with poor scores.

Smith (1966) reported positive but insignificant correlation between achievement and test anxiety whereas Gorblin (1974) and Soman (1977) obtained anxiety as negatively correlated with scholastic achievement. Same has been found by Singh (1974) while studying 200 high school students of both the sexes in rural and urban areas of Ropar district in Punjab.

Kirpal Kaur (1976) and Nair (1980) reported a considerable negative association between the two-anxiety variables and cognitive mathematics' achievement. Kirpal Kaur (1976) further reported that other factors remaining the same and increase in anxiety would tend to decrease congnitive performance in mathematics and vice-versa.

Derstine (1987) also obtained significant relationship between anxiety and academic performance.

The studies show that anxiety has a significant relationship with the school performance of the students. In some it may be negatively related to scholastic achievement while in other cases it is positively related.

Level of Aspiration

Muthayya (1962) and Camerson (1977) found that scholastic achievement was not related to the level of aspiration. The high achievers and low achievers in the scholastic field did not differ significantly in their aspiration patterns. However, Brim et al. (1969) reported that subjects who were most often tested and best informed about their performances were the ones highly motivated to acquire additional information.

Annamalai and Venkata Subramanian (1971) obtained aspiration, educated parents, parental encouragement, absence of financial difficulty, facilities for home study, co-curricular activities and regularity in attendance as helpful to achieve higher scores in high school examination.

Bisht (1972) found a positive relationship between the attainment and the level of educational aspiration. Somehow similar results were obtained by Mohanty (1972) who reported positive and significant relationship between average aspiration scores and examination marks. The high, middle and low achiever groups showed significant difference in their aspiration score before and after performance.

Pandey and Solanki (1975) highlighted that the increased level of aspiration resulted in a significant increase in academic achievement. Level of intelligence had significant effect on academic achievement.

Hussain (1977) found that the academic performance of the group showing moderate goal discrepancy was better than discrepancy was better than that of the groups showing either higher or low goal discrepancy, implying a curvi-linear relationship between the level of aspiration and academic performance.

An insignificant negative correlation (−0.045) was obtained by Madho (1977) but positive and significant (0.286) correlation was reported by Mantro (1979) between academic achievement and student's aspiration. Student's aspiration in case of arts group was higher as compared to that of the science group.

Pal et al. (1985) and Han (1987) also found the level of aspiration as significantly interacting and affecting the scholastic achievements of higher secondary level pupils. Kanitkar (1988) studied the aspirations of decision makers for the education of girls and found very striking differences between the educational aspirations for boys and girls in Bihar in rural as well as urban areas. The aspirations for girls was lower than boys.

Bharti (1990) conducted a study on 300 ninth class students of government and public schools of Chandigarh and reported aspiration level as significantly the performance of the subjects. Performance of high aspiration group was better as comparen to that of low aspiratioq group.

The above mentioned studies show that in some studies level of aspiration is positively related to school performance while some studies show a negative correlation between the level of aspiration and school performance of the students.

3

Methodology

This chapter deals with the methodological steps as adopted for the present investigation. The research procedure followed has been described under the following heads :

Locale of research

Sampling procedure

Variables and their measurement

Tools used for data collection

Data collection

Data analysis

Locale of Research

The study was conducted in Haryana state.

Sampling Procedure

The sampling procedure followed for the study is shown in Fig. 3.1.

Selection of the district : Hisar district of Haryana state was selected purposively as there is lack of such studies in this area and also because of easy accessibility.

Selection of the villages : A cluster of eleven villages of Hisar district having girl students in tenth class were selected by simple random sampling. The villages namely Chirod, Talwandi Rooka, Satroad Kalan and Bhagana fall in Hisar Block-I. Neoli Kalan, Kirtan, Matarsham, Shahpur, Hindwan and Arya Nagar fall in Hisar Block-II. The village Juglan was from Barwala Block (Fig. 3.2).

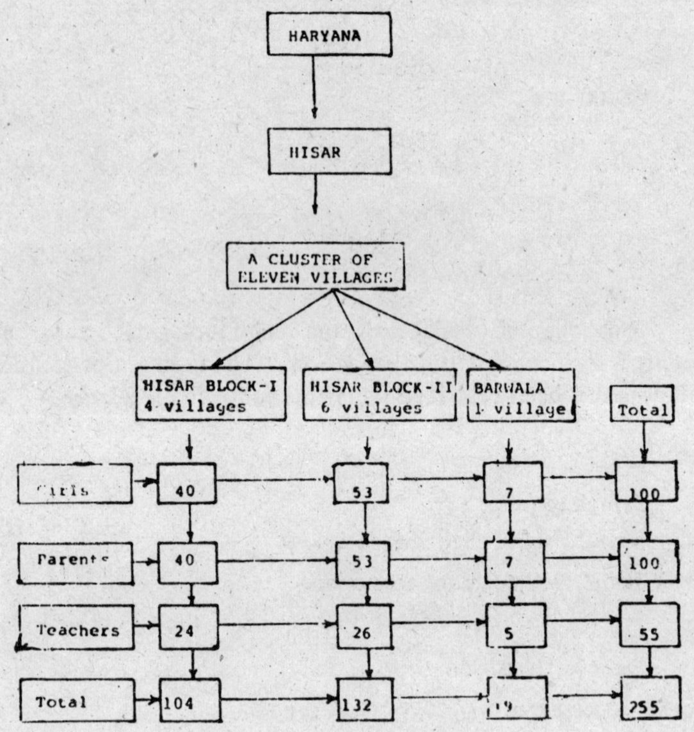

[Fig. 3.1. Sampling Procedure

Selection of respondents : Respondents included 100 girl students studying in class tenth from the eleven villages. Their respective parents and 55 teachers of the students were also selected as respondents. Thus, the total sample size of the study was 255 respondents including girl students, parents and teachers.

Variables and Their Measurement

Dependent variable ; Scholastic achievement was the dependent variable. According to Christian (1980) the academic performance indicates the learning outcome of the students.

Since scholastic achievement refers to the academic performance of the student in the school, the average of the total marks in eighth and ninth classes were taken as the indicator of scholastic achievement of the students.

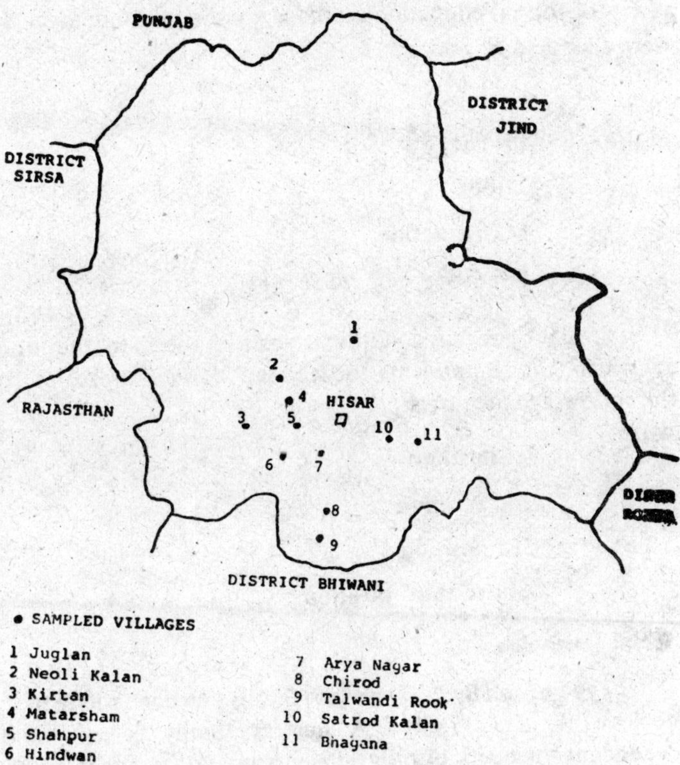

Fig. 3.2. District Map of Hisar.

Independent variables : Personal, social, economic and psychological characteristics were taken as independent variables.

Personal Variables

Age : Age was operationalized as number of full years completed by the respondents at the time of interview who were placed under three different age groups with the number symbol as below :

Below 35 years	1
35-45 years	2
Above 45 years	3

Education . Education was operationalized as number of years of formal education attended by the respondents. These were classified as under :

Illiterate	0
Primary	1
Middle	2
Matriculation	3
Graduate	4

Ordinal position : Ordinal position refers to the number at which the respondents took birth. It was assessed through the following categories :

Ist position	1
2nd position	2
3rd position	3
Above third position	4

Social Variables

Type of family : Type of family means whether it is nuclear of joint family. A nuclear family is composed of dependent members of only one person and its includes minor and other dependents. A joint family refers to one which is constituted by two or more brothers' families. This variable was measured as following :

Nuclear	1
Joint	2

Size of family : Size of family refers to the total number of members in that family whether it is nuclear or joint. The family size was assessed in the following categories :

< 5	1
5-8	2
> 8	3

Number of children : Number of children refers to the total number of living children in that family at the time of investigation, irrespective of their being joint or nuclear. The number of children were categorized as following :

Upto 3	1
4-6	2
> 6	3

Family structure : Family structure refers to the number of boys and girls in the family. Categories were assigned the following numbers :

Only girls	1
Girls with one boy	2
Girls with boys	3
One girl with boys	4
Only one girl	5

Caste : The operational measures of caste was taken from the socio-economic status scale developed by Trivedi (1963). Following numbers were assigned to different caste groups :

Lower (Dhanak, Chamar, Churah)	1
Middle (Dhobi, Khati, Teli, Sunar, Kumhar, Luhar and Nai)	2
Higher (Jat, Rajput, Brahmin and Baniya)	3

Social participation : It refers to the degree to which the parents were involved in formal organizations as members or office bearers. It was adopted as below :

Never a member of any organization	0
Member of one organizaton	1

Socio-economic status : This was operationalized as the total aggregate scores obtained by the individual on a rating scale on the basis of a accumulated score value. Higher the score value, higher would be the socio-economic status and vice-versa. In order to assess the socio-economic status, the Socio-Economic status scale of Kulshreshtha (1980) was used. The categories framed were as below :

Categories	*Scores*
High	Above 110
Medium	60-110
Low	Below 60

Economic Variables

Occupation : This refers to the parents' means of livlihood. Occupations were categorized as below :

Labour	1
Agriculture	2
Petty jobs	3
Service	4
Business	5

Land owned : It refers to the area of cultivable land. possessed by a farm family. Categories assigned were as follows :

No land	0
< 5 acres	1
6-20 acres	2
> 20 acres	3

Annual income : It refers to the total amount of money received by the family through all sources per year. It was operationally measured as per the following :

Rs. < 10,000	1
Rs. 10,000 to 25,000	2
Rs. > 25,000	3

Psychological Variables

Achievement motivation : Operationally achievement motivation has been defined as an inclination of an individual to be concerned with, to plan and to endeavour for circumstances where the performance has to be appraised positively or negatively.

The achievement motivation was assessed by a standardized test of Rao's Achievement Motivation Test (1974). The measurement categories are given as below :

Categories	*Scores*
High Achievement motive	50-60
Average Achievement motive	33-49
Low Achievement motive	20-32

Academic Anxiety

Academic anxiety has been defined as a kind of anxiety which relates to the impending danger from the environments of the academic institutions including teacher, certain subjects like Mathematics, English, Science, etc. Worry about the performance on tests is also a part of it.

The academic anxiety was assessed by a standardized scale of Academic Anxiety (Singh and Gupta, 1984). The measurement categories of the scale were as follows :

Categories	*Scores*
Very anxious	14-20
Moderately anxious	7-13
Less anxious	0-6

Level of Aspiration

Operationally the aspiration level has been defined as the estimate of one's future performance in a given task.

The aspiration level was assessed by a standardized test of level of aspiration (Shah and Bhargava, 1987). Aspiration level was assessed through three types of scores which are given as below :

Attainment Discrepancy Score (ADS) : ADS is the difference between the expected score and the actual score on the same trial. Categories assigned were as follows :

Categories	*Scores*
High aspiration	Mean ADS $> +2$
Average aspiration	Mean ADS $+2$ to -2
Low aspiration	Mean ADS < -2

Goal Discrepancy Score (GDS) : The difference between actual score on the previous trial and goal set up of the next trial is the goal discrepancy score. Categories assigned were as below :

Categories	*Scores*
High aspiration	Mean GDS > 4
Average aspiration	Mean GDS 2 to 4
Low aspiration	Mean GDS < 2

Number of Times Goal Reach Score (NTR) : This is obtained by the number of times where one's actual score is equal or more than the expected score. Categories followed were as below :

Categories	*Scores*
High aspiration	(0 - 3)
Average aspiration	(4 - 7)
Low aspiration	(8 - 10)

Attitude Towards the Girl's Education

It refers to the personal disposition but possessed in different degrees which impel one to react towards the education of girls in ways that can be termed favourable, somewhat favourable, unfavourable. For measurement of attitude a scale was developed by the researcher

Constraints in Girls Education

Constraints refer to the problems or hinderances which the parents, teachers and girls perceived in their education. An interview schedule was prepared for the purpose.

Tools Used for Data Collection

Rao's Achievement Motivation Test (1974)

In this test author retained twently items for the final form to depict achievement range of pupils coming from different socio-economic strata. The final form was administered to a random sample of 550 secondary school pupils of Bhopal. Author has mentioned that though, the test was standardised on the sample of Madhya Pradesh, the nature of the items is such that it can be used in any part of the country. The 20 items of the scale were incomplete sentences, each of which was followed by two possible alternatives A and B which complete the sense. Out of which one was an achievement related item. Though both the alternatives were achievement oriented and socially acceptable, yet one of them imply a higher sense of achievement and excellence.

The coefficient of reliability reported by author is 0.79. The validity is in the form of agreement between the judgement of the teachers and the scores on the achievement motivation test.

Table 3.1

Variables and Their Measurement

S. No.	*Variables*	*Tools used*
A.	**Dependent Variable**	
	1. Scholastic achievement	Average of the total marks in eighth and ninth classes
B.	**Independent Variables**	
	I. Personal variables	Schedule developed
	1. Age	

(*Contd.*)

2. Education	
3. Ordinal position	
II. Social variables	Schedule developed
1. Type of family	
2. Size of family	
3. Number of children	
4. Family structure	
5. Caste	
6. Social participation	
III. Economic variables	Schedule develeped
1. Occupation	
2. Land owned	
3. Annual income	
IV. Socio-Economic Status	SES scale by Kulshreshtha (1980)
V. Psychological variables	
1. Achievement motivation of girls	Rao's Achievement Motivation Scale (1974)
2. Academic Anxiety in Girls	Academic Anxiety Scale by Singh and Gupta (1984)
3. Level of Aspiration of Girls	Level of Aspiration Scale by Singh and Bhargava (1987)
4. Constraints perceived	Schedule developed
(i) by girls	
(ii) by parents	
(iii) by teachers	
5. Attitude of parents and teachers towards girls' education.	Scale developed by researcher

Academic Anxiety Scale for Children (Singh and Gupta, 1984)

This test was administered on a fresh heterogenous sample of 600 students studying in class VIII, IX and X (age range 13-16 years). The test, retest and split half reliability have been reported as 0.60 and 0.65, respectively. The external criteria validity has been reported as 0.41 when validated against Sinha's anxiety test and 0.31 with Neuroticism scale and 0.57 when correlated with CAAT.

Level of Aspiration Scale (Shah and Bhargava, 1987)

This scale was administered on 600 higher secondary and college going male students and percentile norms were established.

The test-retest reliability of this test was 0.82 and split-half 0.69 by ADS score. Reliability by GDS score in test-retest method was 0.88 and by split half method it was 0.77. Reliability by test-retest method according to NTR score was 0.86 and by split half method it was 0.78.

Validity of the Scale

Validity coefficients were found with few tasks and available allied tests of aspirations. All the obtained 'r' values between level of aspiration and different external criteria were found significant at 0.01 level.

Attitude Towards Girls' Education

Measurement of attitude towards girls' education was done with the help of specially developed attitude scale for teachers and parents. The methodological steps followed in the development of scale are as below :

A. Item collection

Fifty five statements related to the content area were collected and reframed. These statements were derived from the relevant literature and discussion with the experts in the field. Statements so prepared were subjected to 30 judges of the relevant fields for rating on the three point scale. The judges were asked to examine the statements for their being relevent, somewhat relevant and not relevant. Only those statements which were marked as relevant by 80 per cent of the judges were retained for further analysis. The selected statements were adminstered to 20 parents and 20 teachers of the tenth class girl students. Their responses were taken on five point scale i.e. strongly agree, agree, undecided, disagree and strongly disagree. These were assigned weightage of 5, 4, 3, 2, and 1, respectively for positive statements and reversed scoring was done for negative statements.

B. Item analysis

Total scores of each respondent were computed by summing up the scores on individual items in array. Twenty five per cent of subjects with the highest and 25 per cent with the lowest total scores formed the criterion group for evaluation of individual statement. The critical ratio (t) was calculated. The critical value of all the statements indicated that these differentiated significantly between high and low groups and hence, were retained in the final scale. Thus, 28 statements selected comprised the final version of the atttiude scale.

Reliability of the Scale

The reliability of the scale was tested by two methods viz., Split half method and test-retest method on a sample of 40 and 20 respondents, respectively. The split-half reliability on odd even items was 0.94 which is highly significant. The test-retest reliability coefficient was 0.99 when tested after a gap of 30 days.

Validity of the Scale

Validity of items was ensured on the basis of significant 't' values obtained earlier. This provided scope of discrimination between statements, hence, measured exactly what was intended to measure.

Constraints' Questionnaire

In order to assess the constraints perceived by parents, teachers and the students in their education, a close ended inventory was prepared. Items regarding personal and community constraints and constraints faced at home or at school were included in the inventory. Three separate inventories having 21 statements for parents, 55 statement for girls and 11 statements for teachers were prepared. Responses were taken under three categories with the following scores:

Categories	*Scores*
Not perceived	0
Rarely perceived	1
Frequently perceived	2

The minimum score on an inventory was zero. The maximum scores on parents' inventory were 42, on girls' inventory were 110 and on teachers' inventory the maximum were 22.

Data Collection

Data were collected personally with the help of various tests inventories and interview schedule as described in preceeding section. These all were pre-tested on a sample of 20 parents, 20 teachers and 20 girl students of class tenth in three villages namely, Gangwa, Muklan and Kaimeri. Necessary modifications were made to make the schedule more functional and field applicable.

Special permission was taken from the school headmastor/headmistress to interview and to test the students. Marks of the students were obtained from the school records. Then girls of tenth class were invited alongwith their pens and a support ing board to write. They were collected in a separate room. Rapport was established with the girl students. This took about 15 minutes. After that the first test of Achievement Motivation was given. Although, instructions were printed on the front page, yet, the students were made clear that they understood all the instructions before starting the test. In 12.15 minutes every student finished the task. Answer-sheets were collected with a word of thanks.

The second test of Academic Anxiety was given after some time gap. Instructions were made clear and after that the test was given to them. In 10 to 15 minutes students finished the task. The answer-sheets were collected.

The 'Level of Aspiration' test was given after a little gap. Instructions were given and made clear. In 15 minutes this test was also finished. Finally, every girl was called individually and was interviewed on constraints which they perceived in their education. Along with this addresses of their parents were taken from the students. In the mean time teachers also filled up and returned their schedules. Then the researcher left the school after giving thanks to the principal, teachers as well as to the students.

Parents were visited to take their opinions regarding girls' education and the constraints perceived in the girls' education. This required a weeks' time. The data collection was completed in three months' time viz., November, 1991 to January 1992.

Data Analysis

The collected data were first tabulated on a master table from which appropriate tables were formulated depending on the kind of formation required keeping in view the objectives of the study. Statistical tools applied are as below:

1. **Percentages.** Simple percentage were calculated to assess the background profile of the respondents.

2. **Reliability coefficients.** Following formula was used to find out the reliability of the attitude scale.

$$r = \frac{\Sigma xy}{\sqrt{\Sigma x^2 x \Sigma y^2}}$$

where,

$$x = x - \bar{x}$$

$$y = y - \bar{y}$$

3. **Critical ratio.** This was used to find out the validity of scale.

$$\text{'t' test} = \frac{\bar{X}_H - \bar{X}_L}{\sqrt{s^2 \left(\frac{1}{n1} + \frac{1}{n2}\right)}}$$

where,

$$S^2 = \frac{(n_1 - 1)\, s^2_1 + (n_2 - 1)\, S^2_2}{n1 + n2 - 2}$$

$\bar{X}_H$ = The mean score of a given statement for the higher group

$\bar{X}_L$ = The mean score of a given statement for the lower group

s^2_1 = The variance of the distribution of responses of higher group

s^2_2 = The variance of the distribution of responses of lower group

n_1 = Number of respondents in high group

n_2 = Number of respondents in low group

4. Chi-square test

Chi-square test was applied to test whether there existed any association between dependent and independent variables. Chi-square was computed by the application of the formula suggested by Michel and Gareth (1968).

Chi-square test (Yate's correction)

$$\text{Chi-square test} = x^2 = \Sigma\Sigma = \frac{[\,|O_{ij} - E_{ij}| - .5]^2}{E_{ij}} \sim (m-1)\,(n-1)\ \text{d.f.}$$

where,

O_{ij} = Observed number of cases categorised in i-th row of j – th column

E_{ij} = Number of cases expected to be categorised in i-th row of j – th column

d.f. = Degree of freedom

m = Number of columns

n = Number of rows

Rank correlation

The principle behind Spearman's measure is to compare the rankings on the two sets of scores.

$$r = 1 - \frac{6\Sigma di^2}{n(n^2-1)}$$

where,

di = Sum of the squares of difference

n = Number of items in the set

4

Results and Discussion

This chapter deals with the results emerging from the investigation. The results on the basis of the objectives of the study have been presented under the following main heads:

- Scholastic achievement of high school girl students
- Perceived constraints and attitude of parents towards girls' education
- General information about the teachers and their attitude and perceived constraints in girls' education
- Scholastic achievements of girls students in relation to socio-personal, economic and psychological factors
- Strategy for enhancing the scholastic achievements of girl students

SCHOLASTIC ACHIEVEMENT

In this section, percentage distribution of the high school (tenth class) girl students as per their achievement have been presented under the following heads:

Average marks obtained in eighth and ninth classes

The data in table 4.1 elucidate the distribution of tenth class girl students according to their average marks obtained in final examinations of eighth and ninth classes.

Fig. 4.1. Scholastic Achievements of Girl Students

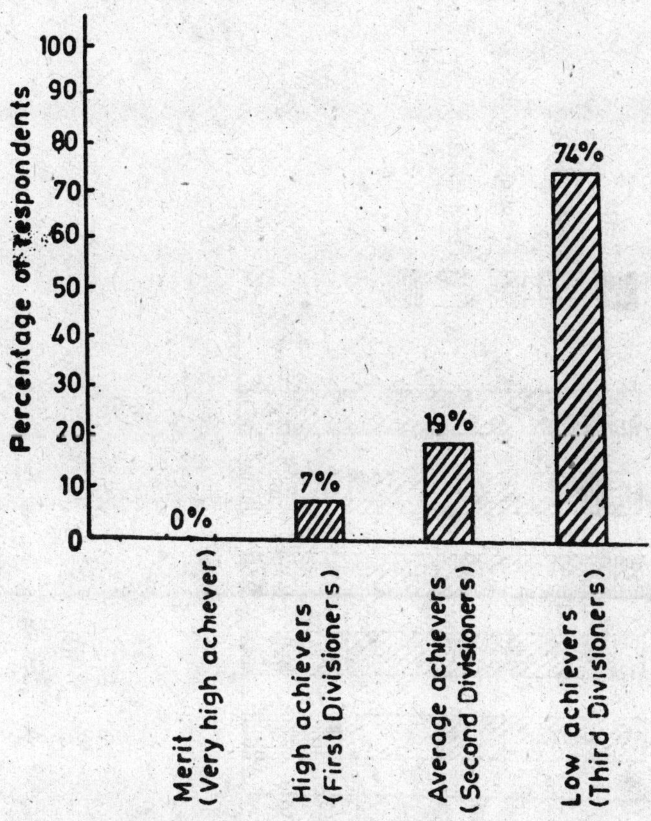

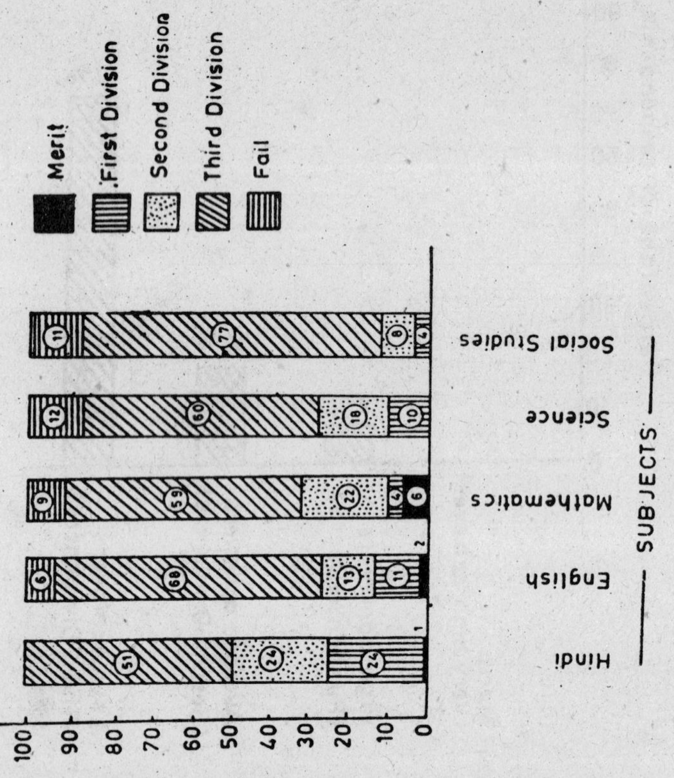

Fig. 4.2. Marks of Girl Students in Different Subjects

TABLE 4.1

Distribution of tenth class girl students according to average marks obtained in eighth and ninth classes

N=100

Division	*Marks Obtained*	*Frequency*
Merit (Very high achiever)	Above 487	0
I (High achiever)	390–487	7
II (Average achiver)	325–389	19
III (Low achiever)	215–324	74

It is depicted in Table 4.1 that majority of the girl students (74%) have obtained third division marks followed by only 19 per cent who obtained second division marks. There were meagre number of girls i.c. 7 per cent having obtained first division marks. There was not a single girl student who obtained merit or marks more than 75 per cent.

The results suggest that the achievement level of the girl students was low. Saroj Bala (1980) also studied the scholastic achievement of high school students and found girls' performance as low. This might be due to many barriers which the rural girls face in their education. The same have been discussed in later section of this chapter. An effort has been made to find out the level of performance on each subject taught to them, so that the root cause of low performance of girls may be explored further.

Performance of respondents subject-wise

Table 4.2 depicts to average marks obtained in different subjects by the girl students in the final examinations of eighth and ninth classes.

The data in Table 4.2 show that performance of the girls is not equal in all the subjects. On some subjects they have performed better and low on other subjects. Third division marks were obtained by the majority of the girls i.e. 51, 68, 59,

60 and 77 per cent in Hindi, English, Mathematics, science and Social Studies, respectively. Second division marks were obtained by the 24, 13, 22, 18 and 8 per cent in Hindi, English, Mathematics, Science and Social Studies, respectively, whereas, 24, 11, 4, 10 and 4 per cent obtained first division marks in Hindi, English, Mathematics, Science and Social studies, respectively. Only a negligible number i.e. 1, 2 and 6 per cent of girl students obtained merit in Hindi, English and Mathematics, respectively. None of the girls obtained merit in Science and Social Studies.

TABLE 4.2

Distribution of girl students according to the average marks obtained in the eight and ninth classes in different subjects

(N=100)

Division	*Hindi*	*English*	*Mathematics*	*Science*	*Social Studies*
Merit (Above 75)	1	2	6	0	0
I (60 to 74)	24	11	4	10	4
II (50 to 59)	24	13	22	18	8
III (33 to 49)	51	68	59	60	77
Fail (below 33)	0	6	9	12	11

The girls who obtained marks less than 33 or who could not obtain the minimum passing marks in the subjects were 12 per cent in Science, 11 per cent in Social Studies, 9 per cent in Mathematics and 6 per cent in English. However, none was fail in Hindi.

Thus, it is evident that most difficult subjects for the girl students were Science and Social Studies followed by Mathematics and English. Hindi was comparatively less difficult for the girl students. Hindi being the mother tongue is easy to comprehend whereas English being the foreign language is not in common use. Moreover, parents being uneducated or less educated cannot provide any assistance. Thus, it becomes difficult for the students to comprehend, grasp and retain the material taught in English.

The poor performance on Science, Social Studies and Mathematics is a matter of great concern because these are taught in students' own language i.e. Hindi. The teaching method is another important component of school education. The way teacher introduces the topic, explains, uses teaching aids, all are important in education. The regular examinations, the classroom atmosphere of mutual understanding between teacher and the student play very crucial role in students' education. Girls being more submissive suffer more. Other factors related to girls' education have been attempted in subsequent sections. The poor school performance of girls affect their continuity in school which ends up in drop outs.

The drop out rate

The drop out rate among the girl students after eighth and ninth classes in the eleven sampled villages is shown below in Table 4.3.

Table 4.3

Drop out among girl students after eighth and ninth classes in eleven sampled villages

Last examination appeared	*Enrolment*	*Number of drop outs*	*Percentage of drop out*
Class VIII	128	18	14.06
Class IX	104	2	1.92

The data in Table 4.3 reveal that out of the total number of girls enrolled in eighth and ninth classes, the drop out rate was higher after eighth class (14.06%) as compared to drop out after ninth class (1.92%).

The reason for the low drop out rate after the ninth class is that only those girls are sent to ninth class whose performance were better in lower classes. Parents want them to continue their schooling after getting admitted into class ninth. This drop out rate was as per the record of the school which may be higher in reality. Whatever drop out rate is, it is a wastage of economic and human resources which needs to be prevented. An attempt has been made to explore the casues of drop outs.

Perceived caused of drop outs

Causes of drop outs as perceived by girl students are shown below in Table 4.4.

Table 4.4

Distribution of girl drop outs according to the causes perceived by the respondents

Causes of dropping	*Frequency*	*Percentage*
Excess load of household work	8	40
Marriage	11	55
Prolonged illness	1	5

The Table 4.4 shows that majority of the drop outs (55%) were due to marriage followed by 40 per cent who dropped due to much involvement in household work. Five per cent dropped out due to discontinuation of studies caused by severe disease. This was reported by the respondents of the study. It can be said that the major reasons of girls' drop out were early marriage and excess load of household work. Thus, socio-cultural and family hinderances are the main causes behind drop outs as reported by the respondents.

Failing Percentage

Percentage of girl respondents failed in eighth and ninth classes have been shown in Table 4.5.

Table 4.5

Percentage of girl respondents failed in eighth and ninth classes

Respondent girls	*Number of girls failed*	*Failed in eighth class*	*Failed in ninth class*	*Number of time failed*
100	15	14	1	Only one time

The Table 4.5 shows out of the total 100 girl respondents of class tenth, 15 girls were those who could reach class tenth after their failure once either is class eighth or class ninth. Out of these 15 girls, 14 girls were failed at their eighth grade examination while one girl was failed at ninth grade examination. It is also a point to be considered that the eighth grade examination is conducted by the board whereas, the ninth grade examination is purely an internal affair.

The above described failure rate among girls might be due to many home, school, community or personal constraints which the rural girls face in their education. The following section deals with the constraints perceived and the attitude of parents towards girls' education.

PERCEIVED CONSTRAINTS AND ATTITUDE

An attempt has been made in the following section to find out the constraints in girls' education as perceived by the girls themselves and their parents and also the attitude of parents towards girls' education. It is essential to understand the family background of the respondents before procceding further. The following section deals with the same.

Family background of girl respondents

In this section, percentage distribution of personal, social and economic characteristics of the parents of the girls have been presented as below:

Personal, Social and Economic Characteristics of Parents

Personal, social and economic characteristics of parents which may be associated with the girls' performance in school ha ve been presented in Table 4.6.

Personal Variables

Mother's age: Majority of the mothers (78%) of the respondents were in the age group of 35 to 45 years. Wheresa only 12 per cent were of the age below 35 years followed by 10 per cent in the age group of above 45 years.

Father's age: Majority of the fathers (77%) of the respondents were in the age group of 35 to 45 years followed by 21 per cent who were above 45 years in age. A negligible number i.e. only 2 per cent were below 35 years.

Table 4.6

Distribution of parents according to their personal, social and economic characteristics

(N=100)

S. No. Variable		*Range*	*Frequency and percentage*
A. Personal Variables			
1.	Mother's age	Below 35 years	12
		35 to 45 years	78
		Above 45 years	10
2.	Father's age	Below 35 years	2
		35 to 45 years	77
		Above 45 years	21
3.	Mother's education	Illiterate	82
		Primary	7
		Middle	5
		Matric	4
		Graduate	2
4.	Father's education	Illiterate	30
		Primary	19
		Middle	8
		Matric	32
		Graduate	11
B. Social Variables			
1.	Family type	Nuclear	87
		Joint	13
2.	Family size	< 5 members	5
		5-8 members	64
		> 8 members	31
3.	Number of children	Upto 3 children	24
		4-6 children	54
		> 6 children	22

(Contd.)

4. Family structure	Only girls	1
	Girls with one boy	15
	Girls with boys	64
	One girl with boys	19
	One girl	1
5. Caste	Lower	10
	Middle	33
	Higher	57
6. Social participation	Never a member of any organisation	90
	Member of one organisation	10
C. Economic Variables		
1. Occupation	Labour	7
	Agriculture	44
	Petty jobs	10
	Service	30
	Business	9
2. Annual income	<10,000	11
	Rs. 10,000-25,000	50
	>Rs. 25,000	39
3. Land owned	No land	15
	<5 acres	28
	5-20 acres	37
	>20 acres	20
D. Socio-Economic Status		
(Scores on Kulshereshtha Test, 1980)	Low SES (Below 60)	60
	Average SES (60-110)	40
	High SES (Above 110)	00

Frequencies are in percentages as 'N' is 100.

Mother's education: Majority of the mothers (82%) were without formal education. Out of remaining 18 per cent, 7 per cent were educated upto primary level, 5 per cent upto middle and 4 per cent upto matriculation level. Only 2 per cent were educated upto graduation level.

Father's education: Almost one-third of fathers i.e. 30 per cent were illiterate aud one-third per cent were educated upto matriculation. Ninteen, and 8 per cent were educated upto primary, graduation and middle level of education, respectively.

Thus, majority of the mothers and fathers of respondents were between the age group of 35 to 45 years. Majority of the mothers were illiterate, whereas, majority of the fathers were educated upto matric. Though one-third of them were illiterate.

Social Variables

Family type: Most of the respondents (87%) belonged to the nuclear families whereas, only 13 per cent belonged to joint families.

Family size: Majority of the respondents (64%) belonged to the families in which there were five to eight members. Only 5 per cent of the respondents belonged to the families in which there were less than five members.

Number of children: More than half of the families (54%) were having four to six children. Whereas, 24 per cent of the families were having three children followed by 22 per cent families having more than six children.

Family structure: Majority of the families (64%) had children of both the sexes. Only 10 per cent of families had several boys with one girl followed by 15 per cent of the families in which there were several girls with one boy. Whereas, one family had several girls only and another one had only one girl and not the boys.

Caste: More than half of the girls (57%) belonged to higher castes followed by 33 per cent from middle castes. However, only 10 per cent girls belonged to lower castes.

Social participation: Fathers of majority of the girls (90%) were never a member of any formal organisation while 10 per cent of them were a member of one formal organisation at least.

Thus, majority of the respondents belonged to nuclear family with five to eight number of members in the family. Majority of the families had four to six number of children who were both boys and girls in the family. Majority of the respondents belonged to higher castes whose fathers were never a member of any formal organisation.

Economic Variables

Occupation: Majority of the fathers (44%) had agriculture as their main occupation. Only 10 per cent were doing service. While the other 10 per cent of the fathers were engaged in small household job followed by 9 per cent engaged in business whereas, 7 per cent of the fathers' were labourers.

Annual income: Half of the respondents (50%) belonged to the families having annual income between Rs. 10,000 to 25,000. Thirty-nine per cent of the families' annual income was more than Rs. 25,000. Only 11 per cent of the families had annual income less than Rs. 10,000.

Land owned: Thirty seven per cent of the families were having land holding of 5 to 20 acres whereas, 28 per cent of the families had land less than 5 acres. Only 20 per cent of families had a land holding more than 20 acres. Remaining 15 per cent of the families had no land.

Socio economic status: More than half of the families (60%) belonged to low socio-economic statue whereas, 40 per cent to average socio-economic status. There was no family from the high socio-economic status.

Thus, majority of the fathers were engaged in agriculture who had annual income of Rs, 10,000 to 25,0C0. Majority of the families had a total land holding of 5 to 20 acres. Majority belonged to low socio-economic status.

Psychological variables of parents

The relevant information regarding some of the psycholgical aspects of the parental thinking has been presented under the following two sub-heads:

Constraints perceived by parents in education of girls

Parents' support to girls' education much depend on the way they perceive the importance of education and also the constraints they face while supporting the education of their daughters. In the following section an attempt has been made to analyse the constraints as perceived by the parents.

The frequency of constraints as perceived by parents in education of girls has been shown in Table 4.7. The constraints have been divided into three categories—home constraints, personal constraints and community constraints.

Home Constraints

Large family size: More than half of the parents (60%) frequently perceived large family size as a constraint in girls' education. While, 35 per cent of the parents rarely perceived and only 5 per cent parents did not perceive large family size as constraint in girls' education.

Low family income: It is evident from the Table 4.7 that 65 per cent of the parents frequently perceived the low family income as a constraint in girls' education. Twenty nine per cent of the parents rarely perceived only 6 per cent did not perceive the low family income as a constraint in girls' education.

Lack of time: Table 4.7 indicates that most of the parents (80%) frequently perceived lack of time as a constraint in their girls' education. Nine per cent of parents rarely perceived the lack of time as a constraint in girls' education whereas 11 per cent parents did not perceive lack of time as a constraint in girls education.

Lack of family assistance in teaching and guiding: It is observed from the Table 4.7 that most of the parents (93%) frequently perceived the lack of family assistance in teaching and guiding as a constraint in girls' education. Only 5 per cent rarely perceived this as a constraint while a negligible number (2%) did not perceive this as a constraint in the education of their girls.

Table 4.7

Distribution of parents according to the constraints perceived in the education of girls

(G=100)

S. No. Constraints	*Frequency*			*Total*
	FP	*RP*	*NP*	
A. Home Constraints				
1. Large family size	60	35	5	100
2. Law family income	65	29	6	100
3. Lack of time	80	9	11	100
4. Lack of family assistance in teaching and guiding	93	5	2	100
5. Family conflicts	8	37	55	100
6. Lack of parental interest in educating girls	79	9	12	100
7. Illness of family members	0	25	75	100
8. Lack of space for study	83	11	6	100
9. Lack of electricity facility at home	9	65	26	100
B. Personal Constraints				
1. Lack of girls' interest in studies	35	60	5	100
2. Health problems of the student	0	11	89	100
3. In-Law's displeasure on continuing education after marriage	8	58	34	100

(Contd.)

4. Lack of faith in fairness in examination	9	36	55	100
5. Limited job opportunities	5	35	60	100
C. Community Constraints				
1. Feeling of guilt while not assisting parents in their work	71	14	15	100
2. Lack of community support in creating conducive environment	12	20	68	100
3. More importance to home and field work	82	10	8	100
4. Less number of girls having attended schools	79	17	4	100
5. Community's preference to activities other than education	21	62	17	100
6. Prevailing insecurity	21	75	4	100
7. Early marriage of girls	89	11	0	100

Frequencies are in percentages as 'N' is 100.

Family conflicts : The data in Table 4.7 reveal that more than half of the parents (55%) did not perceive family conflicts as constraint in girls' education followed by 37 per cent parents who rarely perceived this as a constraint. Only 8 per cent of the parents frequently perceived the family conflicts as a constraint in their girls' education.

Lack of interest in educating girls : The Table 4.7 shows that more than three-fourth of the parents (79%) frequently perceived lack of their interest in educating girls. Nine per cent of the parents rarely perceived this as a constraint in the education of their girls. Only 12 per cent parents did not perceive their lack of interest as a constraint in their girls' education.

Illness of family members : It is evident from Table 4.7 that three-fourth of the parents (75%) did not perceive illness of family members as a constraint in the education of their girls. One-fourth of the parents (25%) rarely perceived this as a constraint. No one perceived this as a frequently occurring constraint.

Lack of space for study : Table 4.7 reveals that most of the parents (83%) did not have separate place to study at home for their girls. Whereas, 11 per cent parents rarely perceived this as a constraint and, only 6 per cent parents had separate place to study at home for their girls.

Lack of light facility at home : Nine per cent of the parents frequently perceived lack of light facility at home as a constraint whereas, 65 per cent rarely perceived this as a constraint. Twenty-six per cent did not perceive lack of light facility at home as a constraint in their girls' education.

Personal Constraints

Lack of girls interest in studies : Thirty five per cent expressed that girls themselves do not take interest in their education, while 60 per cent parents rarely perceived this as a constraint. Only 5 per cent of the parents did not perceive this as a constraint in their girls' education.

Health problems of the students : Majority of the parents (89%) did not perceive health problems of the students as a constraint in their education, whereas, 11 per cent perceived it as a rare constraint. No parent frequently perceived this as a constraint in their daughters' education.

In-Law's displeasure on continuing education after marriage: Thirty four per cent parents did not perceive in-law's displeasure on continuing education of their girls even after marriage, whereas, 58 per cent parents rarely perceived this as a constraint in the education of their girls. Remaining 8 per cent parents frequently perceived this as a constraint in the education of their girls.

Lack of faith in fairness in examination : More than half of the parents (55 %) did not perceive lack of faith of their girls in the fairness in examination. Whereas, 36 per cent parents rarely perceived this as a constraint in their girls' education and 9 per cent parents frequently perceived this as a constraint in education of girls.

Limited job opportunities : Sixty per cent of the parents did not find the fewer chances of job after schooling as any obstacle in girls' education. However, 35 per cent did perceive but occurring rarely and 5 per cent perceived this problem as occurring quite often.

Community Constraints

Feeling of guilt while not assisting parents in their work : About three-fourth of the parents (71%) reported that it is difficult to go against community feelings. The community accepted role of women is home role. Community does not appreciate if a girl sits for study when her parents are working. Such community feelings affects the girls' education. Hence, girls are not able to continue with schooling. Fourteen per cent felt this as a constraint rarely, while 15 per cent of the parents did not perceive this as a constraint at all.

Lack of community support in creating conducive environment : More than half of the parents (68%) did not hold neighbours as responsible for girls' education in creating conducive environment. Twenty per cent perceived it as a constraint occurring rarely whereas 12 per cent found it as a constraint occurring frequently.

More importance given to home/field work : Most of the parents (82%) expressed that due to the community factor that main stress is given to home/field work, girls are not able to study. Ten per cent found it as a constraint occurring rarely while 8 per cent did not find it as a constraint at all.

Uncommon practice in the village : Seventy nine per cent of the parents expressed that since no girl of their community goes to school, it is difficult for them to send their daughter. Hence, it is a constraint in girls' education. Another 17 per cent also felt this as a constraint but occurring rarely. However, 4 per cent parents never perceived this as a problem.

Community's preference to activities other than education : Twenty-one per cent parents frequently perceived the constraint that work other than the education of girls is preferred in their community. However, 62 per cent also felt it but rarely, while 17 per cent parents did not perceive this as a constraint having caused disturbance in girls education.

Prevailing insecurity : Twenty-one per cent of the parents reported that environment in village is not favourable for girls to go to school and study while three-fourth of the parents (75%) rarely felt this as a constraint. Only 4 per cent of parents did not find this as a problem at all.

Early marriage of girls : Early marriage of girls has been perceived as a frequently occurring constraint by majority of the parents (89%). The remaining 11 per cent also found it as a constraint but happening rarely. There was no parent who did not perceive this as a constraint.

Thus, it is clear that there were number of constraints perceived by parents. Out of the various home constraints lack of family assistance in teaching and guiding, lack of separate study place, lack of time and lack of parental interest were the major constraints as perceived by the parents. Lack of family assistance in teaching and guiding was perceived as a constraint by majority of the parents in their girls' education. As the majority of the parents of girl respondents were themselves illiterate, it is useless to expect them to teach and guide their wards. Those who could teach and guide were not doing so specially in case of girls because either they themselves were busy or girls were being involved in various home activities. The similar findings have been given by Ismail (1975) who observed that the school work was hard to combine with household chores and said that when little girls found some time for their studies, they were called away by their mothers to attend to some domestic work.

Lack of space for study was also one of the problems as perceived by most of the parents. The same constraint in education of children was found by Saroj Bala (1980) and Contractor (1984). It might be due to the reason that though, the houses in villages are not small yet, they are built in such a way that they provide minimum separate space for study.

Lack of time for studies was also a major problem for girl students. This is because the girls have to help their parents in domestic work, bringing-up younger children and assisting parents in their occupation. This finds the support of Muralidharan (1980), Saroj Bala (1980), Sudha and Tiwari (1985) and Bhaskaran (1989).

Most of the parents were not interested in educating their daughters specially upto higher level. This may be due to traditional and conservative mental make-up of parents, apprehension of insecurity by parents and also the assistance which the parents expect from their daughters. The similar observations were made by Khanna (1977) and Bhaskaran (1989).

Personal constraints are those constraints which are related to the girls themselves. If the learners themselves are not prepared or strongly motivated to achieve the excellence whatever efforts are made by others may not be sufficient for their success. Following section deals with some of such constraints as perceived and reported by the parents

Lack of interest of girl respondents was found one of the major personal constraint of girls perceived by their parents as affecting their performance. Similar constraints were obtained by Khanna (1977) and Skiera (1990) for the low achievement of studedts. This might be due to the reason that girls know that they would not be sent for higher education and they would be married soon after the completion of tenth grade studies at the most. Due to this concept built in minds of girls, neither they work hard and show interest in studies nor, their parents take interest in their daughters' studies. Hence, good achievement from girls is far away. The other two constraints *viz.*, limited job opportunities and lack of faith in fairness in examination did not find much support from the parents. Probably because putting girls into professional career is not their aim because of traditional line of thinking. Since the girls are to be married in their early age and in-laws in general do not permit their daughter-in-laws to go for education, putting unnecessary pressure on girls for achieving excellence will be sheer burden and wastage of time and money both. The other two components of personal constraints like health problem of students and use of unfair means by students in examination was not apprehended by the parents.

As regards community constraints, it has been observed that it is difficult for a person to go against the traditions and customs of the community to which they belong. This affects their social status in community. Some of the such important constraints have been reported by the parents.

The system of early marriages of girls is prevalent in their community. This affects their studies. They do not get much interested in their studies because they begin to think and to dream about their marriage and after marriage life. It is difficult for the parents to go against the advice of the community and to take decisions against their wishes. Girls just surrender to the wishes and expectations of parents and the community. If girl is married during her academic session, her in-laws would not permit her to complete the same academic year. This is a sort of community pressure under which girls are made to suffer. Similar observations were reported by Pillai (1975) and Talesra (1986).

Further, it is a common practice in the village community that a girl is appreciated more if she supports her parents either by working in the home or helping them in their field activities. If a girl spends more time on her studies, it is generally viewed negatively. The same has been observed in the present etudy. It has been found that due to the more importance given to home/field work in villages and not to the education specially in case of girls, their studies are adversely affected. The same has been supported by Ojha (1966) and Bhaskaran (1989) who obtained similar results. The community value system might have been developed due to the poverty because of which parents engage their children in home/field work to support their family income. Education of children becomes a wastage for them. Historically viewing the social security may be one of the reasons for confining girls to home roles. This might have got in-built in the cultural practices which took the form of tradition to prepare the girls for home role right from the beginning. Education is considered secondary that even, only for fulfilling the home roles efficiently.

It has been found in this study that very less number of girls are going to school in villages. No one has courage to go to school outside the village. Even their parents do not allow them to go alone outside. This might be due to the reason that parents feel their girls insecure when they go outside the home. Due to the general opinion and attitude of the community as a whole, the girls' education is affected. Similar reasons were found by Bhandari (1982).

In village community, girls feel guilty while studying instead of assisting parents in their work. This might be due to the reason that parents and the community expect their girls to devote their time primarily in domestic work/field work or assisting them in other occupations. Hence, the domestic work, the field work and the parental occupation become a major constraint in village community leading to lack of time for the studies of children. Mani (1980) made similar observations that such constraints affect girls' education.

Constraint scores

The data in Table 4.8 show the score distribution on constraints as obtained by the parents. Three categories with the equal range of scores have been devised between the highest and the lowest scores obtained by the respondents. These three categories are designated as low constraints, medium constraints and high constraints. The main purpose of calculating the scores on constraints was to find out correlation between constraints in education and the scholastic achievement of girls. The frequency of respondents in differe t categories have been described as follows :

H(me constraints. Fourty four per cent parents were classified as having perceived home constraints at low level,

Table 4.8.

Distribution of parents according to scores obtained on constraints in girls' education

(N =100)

S. No.	*Variables*	*Score Range*	*Frequency*
1.	**Home constraints**		
	Low	6-9	44
	Medium	10-12	28
	High	13-16	28
2.	**Personal constraints**		
	Low	0-3	25
	Medium	4-6	62
	High	7-9	13
3.	**Community constraints**		
	Low	6-8	1
	Medium	9-11	35
	High	12-14	64
4.	**Composite constraint scores**		
	Low	15-22	14
	Medium	23-29	54
	High	30-36	32

Frequencies are in percentages as 'N' is 100

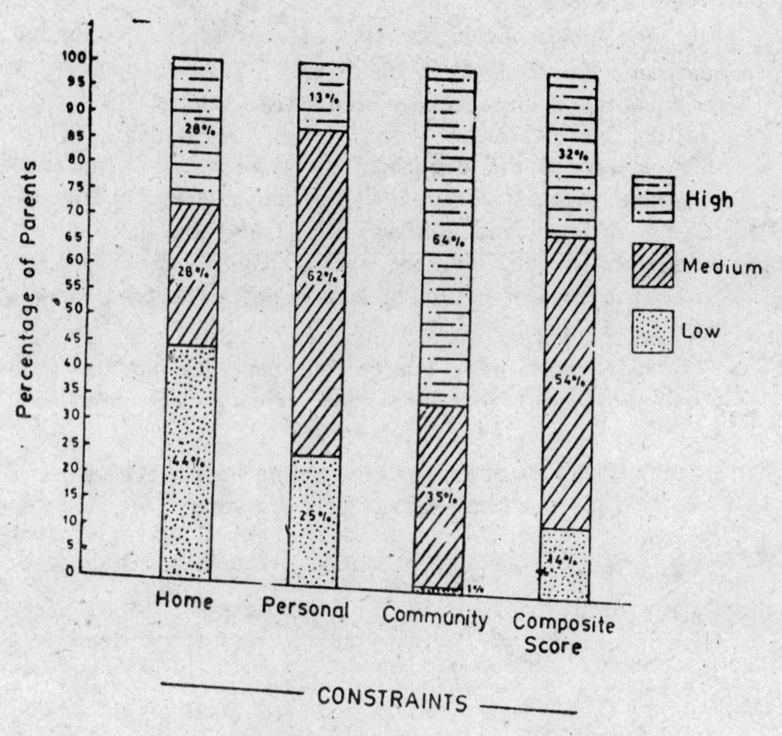

Fig. 4.3. Constraints Perceived by Farents in Girls Education.

28 per cent in middle category and the same percentage in high level category of home constraints.

Personal constraints. More than half of the parents (62%) had perceived personal constraints at medium level and 25 per cent had low level of constraints, while 13 per cent parents had high level of personal constraints of girls affecting their education.

Community constraints. Majority of the parents (64%) had high level of community constraints followed by 35 per cent who had medium level of constraints. A negligible number i.e. only one parent had a low level of community constraints in the education of girls.

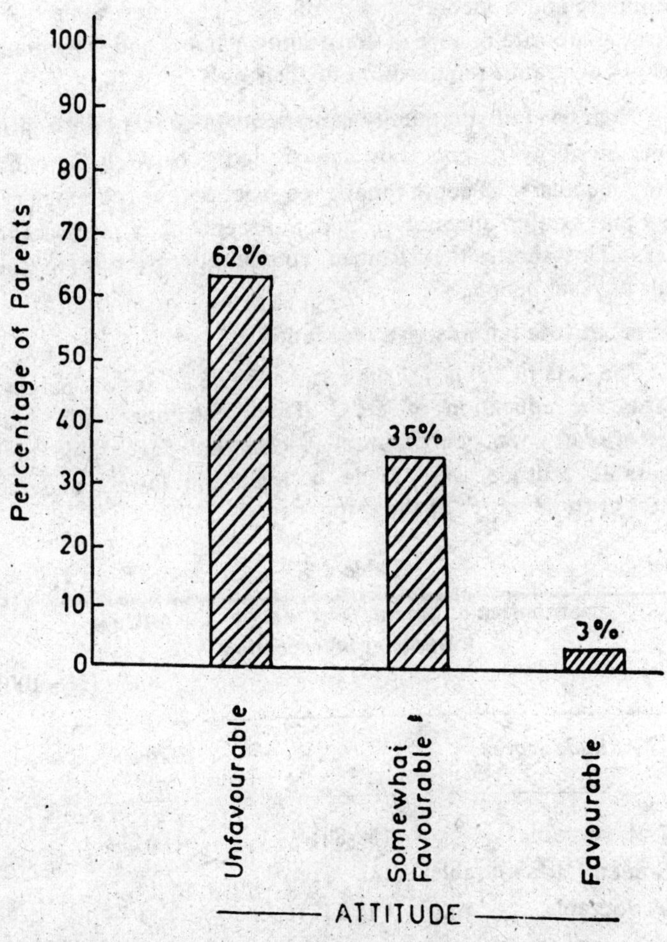

Fig. 4·4. Attitude of Parents Towards Girls' Education.

Composite constraint scores. More than half of the parents (54%) had medium level of constraints, in general. Thirty-two per cent had high level of constraints and only 14 per cent had low level of constraints in the education of girls.

It may be concluded, therefore, that majority of the parents had low level of home constraints but a high level of community and a medium level of personal constraints. As regards composite picture of constraints, parents had a medium level of constraints in education of their girls.

High level of community constraints in education of girls as perceived by parents show the strong ties between the community members. People cannot go against the community. They may suffer themselves and put their family members to suffer. This shows the stronger community pressure in the minds of rural people.

Parents' attitude towards girls' education

The data in Table 4.9 show the attitude scores of parents towards the education of girls. Three categories with equal range of scores *viz.*, unfavourable, somewhat favourable and favourable attitude were made between the lowest and the highest attitude scores of the respondents.

Table 4.9

Distribution of parents according to the attitude towards girls' education

(N = 100)

Attitude scores		*Frequency*
Unfavourable	(68-82)	62
Somewhat favourable	(83-97)	35
Favourable	(98-112)	3

Table 4.9 indicates that majority of the parents 62%) had unfavourable attitude towards the education of girls

followed by 35 per cent parents who had somewhat favourable attitude. Only 3 per cent parents had favourable attitude towards girls' education.

Attitude is a force which mobilizes the human action for or against. The negative attitude of parents as shown in the table is a clear indication that girls' education would not be supported by them.

Information about girl student respondents

The relevant information regarding girls' performance on their various psychological tests and constraints perceived in education along with an important related family variable has been presented below :

Ordinal position of girls

The ordinal position of girls have been shown as below in Table 4.10.

Table 4.10

Distribution of girl respondents according to their birth position

(N=100)

Birth position	*Frequency*
I	32
II	20
III	23
> III	25

The data in Table 4.10 indicate that majority of the girl respondents (32%) had first birth position. The remaining respondents almost with an equal distribution i.e. 25 per cent had position above third, 23 per cent had third birth position and 20 per cent had second birth or ordinal position in her family.

This information may be relevant in finding the effect of birth related factors on achievement level of respondents which has been attempted and described under the heading 'scholastic achievements of girl students in relation to socio-personal, economic and psychological factors'.

Performance on psychological tests

The data in Table 4.11 have been discussed under the following heads :

Academic anxiety. Majority of the girl respondents (60%) were moderately anxious followed by 29 per cent who were very anxious. Only 11 per cent of the girl respondents were less anxious.

Achievement motivation. Majority of the girl respondents (57%) were classified as having high achievement motivation whereas, respondents almost with an equal number i.e. 22 per cent had average and 21 per cent girl respondents had low level of achievement motivation.

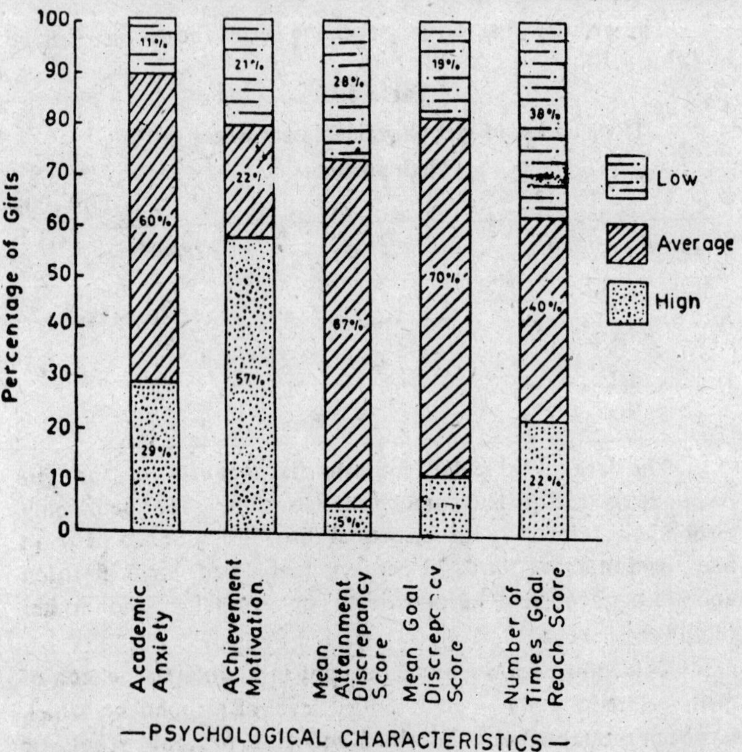

Fig. 4.5. Psychological Characteristics of Girls.

Aspiration level. Aspiration level of the girl respondents was assessed through three types of scores as follows :

Attainment discrepancy score (ADS). According to this score majority of the girl respondents i.e. 67 per cent had average level of aspiration followed by 28 per cent who had low level of aspiration. Only 5 per cent girl respondents obtained high level of aspiration.

Goal discrepancy score (GDS). According to Goal Discrepancy Score, majority of the respondents (70%) had average level of aspiration and 11 per cent girl respondents had obtained high level of aspiration. Whereas, 19 per cent had low level of aspiration.

Table 4.11

Distribution of girl respondents according to psychological characteristics

S. No.	*Variables*	*Range*	*Frequency*
1.	Academic Anxiety (Academic Anxiety scale by Singh and Gupta, 1984)	Very anxious (14-20)	29
		Moderately anxious (7-13)	60
		Less anxious (0-6)	11
2.	Achievement Motivation (Rao's Achievement Motivation Scale, 1974)	Low Achievement Motive (20-32)	21
		Average Achievement Motive (33-49)	22
		High Achievement Motive (50-60)	57

Contd.

3. Aspiration level (Level of Aspiration Scale by Singh and Bhargawa, 1987)		
(a) Mean Attainment Discrepancy Score (ADS)	Mean ADS $\geq +2$ (High aspiration)	5
	Mean ADS $+2$ to -2 (Average aspiration)	67
	Mean ADS ≤ -2 (Low aspiration	28
(b) Mean Goaal Discrepancy Score (GDS)	Mean GDS ≥ -0.2 (High aspiration)	11
	Mean GDS -0.2 to $+4.1$ (Average aspiration)	70
	Mean GDS $\leq +4.1$ (Low aspiration)	19
(c) Number of times Goal Reach Score (NTR)	Low Aspiration (0-3)	38
	Average aspiration (4-7)	40
	High Aspiration (8-10)	22

Frequencies are in percentages as 'N' is 100

Number of times goal reach score (NTR). According to NTR score 40 per cent respondents had average level of aspiration followed by 38 per cent respondents who had low level of aspiration. The remaining 22 per cent had high level of aspiration.

Through these psychological traits it may be concluded that though the majority of respondents had high achievement motivation, yet, they were moderately anxious and had average level of aspiration for achievement. The information regarding psychological traits is important for finding their impact on scholastic achievement which is discussed in later sections of this chapter.

Constraints perceived by girl respondents

Under this section data have been presented as under :

Frequency distribution of girl respondents according to constraints perceived in education

The data in Table 4.12 reveal the constraints as perceived by girls in their education. These constraints have been classified as under :

HOME CONSTRAINTS

Large family size. Majority of the girl respondents (65%) frequently perceived the large family size as a hinderance in their scholastic achievement. Thirty per cent rarely perceived this as a constraint and 5 per cent of the girl respondents did not perceive this at all as a constraint in their education.

Table 4.12

Distribution of respondents according to perceived constraints in education

(N=10ↄ)

S. No.	Constraints	Frequency FP	RP	NP	Total
A.	**Home constraints**				
1.	Large family size	65	30	5	100
2.	Low family income	60	32	8	100
3.	Lack of time	88	12	0	100
4.	Lack of family assistance in teaching and guiding	96	4	0	100
5.	Family conflicts	7	48	45	100
6.	Lack of parental positive attitude	84	9	7	100
7.	Prolonged illness of family members	0	24	76	100

Contd.

8.	Lack of separate study place	82	12	6	100
9.	Lack of proper light facility	11	65	24	100
B.	**School constraints**				
1.	Poor physical facilities				100
	– Poor classroom physical facilities	14	36	50	100
	– Lack of drinking water facility	0	5	95	100
	– Lock of toilet facility	0	11	89	100
	—Lack of library facility	57	33	10	100
2.	Expensive schooling				
	—Fees	0	0	100	100
	– Clothing	0	7	93	100
	– Books	0	12	88	100
3.	Non-availability of books				
	– Non-availability at shops	0	18	82	100
	– Not available in library	57	33	10	100
	– Inability to purchase	5	22	73	100
4.	Staff facility				
	—Lack of teachers	22	32	46	100
	– Lack of lady teachers	45	35	20	100
	– Lack of teachers' interest in studies	26	59	15	100
	—Teachers rude behaviour	35	49	16	100
	—Teachers stress on private tuition	0	12	88	100
	– Duty delegation to students	5	26	69	100
	—Teachers getting personal work done by the students	0	5	95	100
	– Conflict among teachers	4	12	84	100
	—Unfair judgement by the —Teachers	0	7	93	100

(Contd.)

5. Curriculum problems				
—Difficulty in proper grasp of the subject matter	93	7	0	100
—Non-interesting presentation of material in books	89	11	0	100
—Heavy work load	0	7	93	100
—Over crowding in each class	11	7	84	100
—More time spent on games	0	0	100	100
—Lack of pre-hand preparations	20	35	45	100
—Non-interesting teaching methods	11	40	49	100
6. Other school problems				
—Corporal punishment	0	8	92	100
—Indiscipline caused by boys	76	19	5	100
—Indulgence of students in quarrels	35	49	16	100
—Long distances between residence and school	0	0	100	100
—Non-conducive school environment	7	55	38	100
—Faulty examination system	20	35	45	100
C. Personal constraints				
1. Lack of interest in studies	25	65	10	100
2. Health problem of the student	0	6	94	100
3. Early marriage and parents-in-law's negative attitude towards education	7	55	38	100

Contd.

4. Internal inhibition while asking questions in classroom	92	6	2	100
5. Lack of parental support and encouragement	87	10	3	100
6. Lack of faith in unfair examination system	24	26	50	100
7. Lack of job opportunities	26	51	23	100
D. Community constraints				
1. Community's disapproval of a girl's sitting and studying while parents are at work	86	14	0	100
2. More importance to home and field work	91	9	0	100
3. Lack of community support	15	17	68	100
4. Less number of girls attending schools	76	20	4	100
5. Other girls of community being involved in household work	10	62	28	100
6. Insecurity for the girls	9	51	40	100
7. Early marriage of girls	82	12	6	100

Frequencies are in percentages as 'N' is 100

Low family income. Majority of the girls (60%) frequently perceived followed by 32 per cent who rarely perceived the low family income as a constraint in education of girls. However, 8 per cent did not perceive this as a constraint.

Lack of time Most of the girl respondents (88%) frequently perceived the lack of time as a constraint in education of girls. Remaining 12 per cent rarely perceived the lack of time as a constraint in education of girls. There was no girls respondent who did not perceive this as a constraint.

Lack of family assistance in teaching and guiding. Most of the girls (96%) frequently perceived that there was a lack of family assistance in teaching and guiding. Remaining 4 per cent also perceived this as a constraint but rarely. There was no girl respondent who did not perceive this as a constraint in their education.

Family conflicts. Forty five per cent of girls did not perceive the family conflicts as a constraint in education of girls. But 48 per cent rarely perceived and 7 per cent frequently perceieved the family conflicts as a constraint in their education.

Lack of Parental positive attitude. Eighty four per cent of girl respondents frequently perceived the lack of parental positive attitude towards girls' education, 9 per cent perceived it rarely while 7 per cent did not perceive lack of parental positive attitude towards girls' education as a constraint.

Prolonged illness of family members. Majority of the girl respondents (76%) did not perceive illness of family members as a constraint in their education. Remaining 24 per cent perceived this constraint rarely. There was no respondent who perceived this constraint as occurring frequently.

Lack of separate study place. Majority of the girls (82%) frequently perceived the lack of separate place to study at home as a constraint. However, 12 per cent rarely perceived and 6 per cent girls did not perceive at all the lack of separate space for studies at home as a constraint in their education.

Lack of proper light facility at home. Eleven per cent of the girl respondents frequently perceived the lack of light facility at home as a constraint in their education, whereas, 65 per cent perceived this constraint as occurring rarely. Only 24 per cent of girl respondents did not perceive the lack of light facility at home as a constraint in their education.

SCHOOL CONSTRAINTS

Poor Physical Facilities

Poor classroom physical facilities. Half of the girl respondents (50%) did not perceive the poor classroom physical facilities, whereas, 36 per cent rarely perceived and 14 per cent frequently perceived the poor classroom physical facilities as a constraint.

Lack of drinking water facility. Lack of drinking water was not a frequent constraint in education of girls. Though majority (95%) did not perceive this as a constraint, only 5 per cent perceived this as a constraint that even occurring rarely.

Lack of toilet facility. cack of toilet facility was also not a frequent constraint in education of girls. Eighty nine per cent did not perceive this as a constraint. However, 11 per cent perceived the lack of toilet facility as a constraint occurring rarely.

Lack of library facility. More than half of the respondents (57%) frequently perceived the lack of library facility in school as a constraint. Thirty three per cent perceived this constraint as occurring rarely and only 10 per cent did not perceive the lack of library facility in school as a constraint.

Expensive Schooling

Fees. Fees is not a constraint for girls in rural areas because Haryana Government has made education free for girls upto graduation.

Clothing. Clothing was also not a frequent problem for girls. Ninety three per cent of girl respondents did not perceive clothing as a constraint in their education. However, 7 per cent perceived this constraint as occurring rarely.

Books. Books as being expensive was not a frequent problem for the girl respondents. Seven per cent of girl respondents perceived the expense of books as a constraint occurring rarely whereas, 93 per cent did not perceive this as a constraint in education of girls.

Non-availability of Books

Not available at shops. Non-availabilily of books at shops was not a frequent constraint in education of girls. Majority of the girl respondents (82%) did not perceive this as a constraint. Those who perceived (18%) expressed the problem as occurring rarely.

Non-availability in library. Majority of the girl respondents (57%) frequently perceived the non-availability of books in the school library. Thirty three percent perceived this as a constraint occurring rarely. Only 10 per cent did not perceive the non-availability of books in the library as a constraint.

Inability to purchase. Majority of the girl respondents (73%) did not perceive whereas 5 per cent frequently perceived and 22 per cent rarely perceived the inability to purchase the books as a constraint in their education.

Staff Facility

Lack of teachers. About half of the girl respondents (46%) did not perceive and out of the remaining respondents, 22 per cent frequently perceived and 32 per cent rarely perceived the lack of teachers in the school as a constraint in their education.

Lack of lady teachers. About half of the respondents (45%) frequently perceived the lack of lady teachers in the school and 35 per cent perceived this problem as occurring rarely. Only 20 per cent did not perceive this problem in the education of girls.

Lack of teachers' interest in studies. More than half of the girl respondents (59%) rarely perceived the lack of teachers' interest in studies, 26 per cent frequently perceived and only 15 per cent did not perceive the lack of teachers' interest in studies as a constraint.

Teachers' rude behaviour. About half of the respondents (49%) rarely perceived the teachers' rude behaviour while 35 per cent frequently perceived and only 16 per cent did not perceive teachers' rude behaviour as a constraint in the education of the girls.

Teacher's stress on private tuition. Majority of the girl respondents (69%) did not perceive the problem of teacher's stress on private tuition and 26 per cent perceived this problem as occurring rarely. Only 5 per cent frequently perceived the problem of teachers's stress on private tuition as a constraint in their education.

Duty delegation to students. It has been observed that some times now teachers do not attend duty themselves rather rely upon the monitors of the class and ask them to conduct the teaching classes. Those monitors may or may not behave properly with the students. He may be strict with students due to disciplinary problem or he may be ignorant about the subject matter and teaching methods. However, most of the girl respondents (88%) did not perceive the problem that teachers rely on monitors. The remaining 12 per cent perceived this problem as occurring rarely and none perceived this problem as occurring frequently.

Teachers getting personal work done by the students. Most of the girl respondents (95%) did not perceive the problem of teachers getting personal work done by the students as a hinderance in their studies. The remaining 5 per cent perceived this problem as occurring rarely and nobody perceived this as a frequent problem.

Conflict among teachers. Most of the girl respondents (84%) did not perceive the conflict among teachers in school as a constraint in girls' education. Twelve per cent perceived this as a constraint occurring rarely and 4 per cent frequently perceived the conflict among teachers as a constraint in girls' education.

Unfair judgement by the teachers. Most of the girl respondents (93%) did not perceive the unfair judgement by the teachers whereas, the remaining 7 per cent perceived this problem as occurring rarely. Nobody perceived it as occurring frequently.

Curriculum Problem

Difficulty in proper grasp of the subject matter. Majority of the respondents i.e. 93 per cent frequently perceived difficulty in proper grasp of the subject matter as a constraint. The remaining 7 per cent also perceived this problem but occurring rarely.

Non-interesting presentation of material in books. In this case also every body complained against the presentation of material in the books. Majority of them i.e. 89 per cent frequently perceived and rest of the 11 per cent rarely perceived this as a problem in their education.

Heavy work load. No body perceived frequently the heavy work load as against seven per cent who rarely perceived and 93 per cent who did not perceive this as a problem in their education.

Over-crowding in each class. Eleven per cent frequently perceived over-crowding of students in each class while 5 per cent perceived this problem as occurring rarely. Eighty four per cent did not perceive over-crowding of students in each class as a problem in their education.

More time spent on games. No body perceived that more time is spent on games than on studies as hindering the studies of girl students.

Lack of pre-hand preparations. Twenty per cent frequently perceived that there was lack of pre-hand preparations of lessons by teachers. While 35 rer cent perceived this problem as occurring rarely and about half of the girl respondents (45%) did not perceive this as a constraint.

Non-interesting teaching method. Eleven per cent frequently perceived that the method of teaching (of teachers) was not interesting while 40 per cent perceived it as occurring rarely. Nearly half of the girl respondents (49%) did not perceive this problem as a constraint in their education.

Other School Problems

Corporal punishment. Nobody perceived corporal punishment as a constraint occurring frequently in the education of girls in the school. Eight per cent perceived this constraint occurring rarely while most of the respondents (92%) did not perceive this as a problem in girls' education.

Indiscipline caused by boys. Majority of the girl respondents (76%) frequently perceived that indiscipline is caused by boys in school. Ninteen per cent perceived this problem as occurring rarely while 5 per cent did not perceive indiscipline in the school, caused by boys.

Indulgence of students in quarrels. Thirty five per cent frequently perceived the indulgence of students in quarrels while about half of the girl respondents (49%) perceived this problem as occurring rarely. Sixteen per cent respondents did not perceive this as a constraint.

Long distance between residence and school. Nobody perceived this constraint because all the respondents were studying in the schools situated in their own villages.

Non-conducive school environment. Seven per cent respondents frequently perceived the non conducive environment in the school for studies. While more than half of the girl respondents (55%) perceived this constraint as occurring rarely. However, thirty eight per cent did not perceive this as a problem in their studies.

Faulty examination system. Twenty per cent of the girl respondents frequently perceived the faulty examination system as a constraint in their education. Whereas 35 per cent perceived this constraint as occurring rarely and nearly half of the respondents (45%) did not perceive this as a constraint.

PERSONAL CONSTRAINTS

Lack of interest in studies. Twenty five per cent of the girl respondents frequently perceived the lack of their own interest in studies as a factor causing constraint in their studies. Majority of the respondents (65%) perceived it as occurring rarely. while 10 per cent did not perceive the lack of their own interest in studies as a constraint in their education.

Health problems of the student. Most of the girl respondents (94%) did not perceive their prolonged illness hindering in studies while remaining 6 per cent percerived this problem as occurring rarely and nobody perceived it as occurring frequently.

Early marriage and parent-in-laws' negative attitude towards education. Seven per cent frequently perceived the early marriage and parent-in-laws' negative attitude towards their education. Whereas, 55 per cent perceived this problem as occurring rarely. Thirty eight per cent did not perceive this problem as a hinderance in their education.

Internal inhibition while asking questions in classroom. Most of the girl respondents i.e. 92 per cent had frequent internal inhibition while asking questions in classroom. Six per cent perceived this constraint as occurring rarely. A negligible number i.e. 2 per cent did not perceive this problem.

Lack of parental support and encouragement: Majority of the respondents (87%) frequently perceived the lack of parental support and encouragement for their studies while 10 per cent perceived this problem as occurring rarely. Only 3 per cent did not perceive this as a problem in their education.

Unfair examination system: Half of the respondents (50%) did not lack the faith in fairness in examination system. However, twenty four per cent frequently perceived and twenty six per cent rarely perceived the use of unfair means and unfair marking system in examinations as causing constraint in their education.

Lack of job opportunities. Twenty six per cent respondents frequently perceived and 51 per cent rarely perceived the lack of the job opportunities as causing constraint in their studies. Twensy three per cent did not perceive this as a problem.

COMMUNITY CONSTRAINTS

Community's disapproval of a girl sitting and studying while parents are at work: Majority of the girl respondents (86%) frequently felt the community's disapproval of a girl sitting and studying while parents were working as causing constraint in their education. The remaining 14 per cent also perceived this problem as occurring rarely.

More importance to home and field work: All the respondent perceived this as a contraint in their education. Most of the girl respondents i.e. 91per cent frequently perceived and the remainig 9 per cent perceived this constraint as occuring rarely. Infact when neighbours or family visitors criticise the girl for not helping the parents in their work, it becomes difficult for them to go against the community expectations, which may ultimately mount constraint in girls' education.

Lack of community support: Majority of the girl respondents (68%) did not perceive the lack of community support in creating conducive environment for carrying schooling by girls. Fifteen per cent frequently perceived and 17 per cent rarely perceived this as a constraint.

Less number of girls attending schools: Majority of the girl respondents (76%) frequently perceived that very less number of girls go to schools which may give the feeling of lonelines among the girls. Twenty per cent perceived this constraint as occuring rarely and only 4 per cent did not perceive this as a constraint.

Other girls of community being involved in household work: Ten per cent of girl respondents frequently perceived that when other girls in the community are busy with household and other related work, their interest in studies diminishes. However, 62 per cent perceived this constraints as occurring rarely and twenty eight per cent did not perceive this as a constraint in their education.

Insecurity for the girls. Nine per cent respondents frequently perceived that there prevails insecurity for the girls in the villages. The bad elements of the villages may create unpleasant situation or even fear in the minds of the parents regarding the safety of the girls. More than half (51%) of the girl respondents perceived it occurring rarely and forty per cent did not perceive this contraint at all.

Early marriage of girls : Majority (12%) of the girl respondents frequently perecived that there exists a custom of early marriages of girls in their community which is causing hinderance in their studies. Another 12 per cent perceived this constraint as occurring rarely, whereas, 6 per cent did not perceive this as a constraint.

This may be concluded from Table 4.12 that major home constraints and the community constraints as perceived by girl respondents in their education were same as the constraints which were perceived by their parents in girls' education. There is a little difference of frequency only. The major home constraints were lack of family assistance in teaching and guiding, lack of time for studies, lack of parental positive attitude and lack of separate study space at home. The major community constraints were, more importance given to home and field work, community's disapproval of a girl sitting and studying while parents were working, less number of girls going to school and early marriages of girls.

Out of the school constraints, lack of library facility for loaning books was found one of the major school problems as perceived by majority of the girls respondents. This result finds the support of Shukla (1983) who found the lack of physical facilities including the library facility affecting the scholastic success and progress of students. This has been observed during the visits of the schools that the books from the school library are provided free of cost to the girls belonging scheduled castes/backward castes. The students belonging to higher castes were also in the need of books which they were not getting.

Limited number of lady teachers in the sehool was one of the major staff problem as perceived by majority of the girl respondents. Rai (1975) and Shah (1991) also found the similar results. In fact, due to scarcity of female teachers in the rural schools, neither the parents are interested to send their daughters to schools nor the girls themselves find comfortable in the classes conducted by male teachers.

Majority of the girl respondents also reported the non-interesting presentation of material in books and causing difficulty in proper grasp of the subject matter. Similar findings were reported by Ismail (1975), Daniel (1976) and Skiera (1990), who stressed upon preparing the books in more appropriate manner so as to generate interest in readers. It is the defective system of teaching mainly responsible for poor performance. In fact the school education did not satisfy the psycho-economic and social needs of the students. School education is also not well designed to deal with the students individually.

Indiscipline in the school as caused by boys was another major problem as perceived by girl respondents. Co-education causes some indiscipline responsible for low interest of girl students in studies. Other constraints as listed in Table 4.12 did not find much support from the respondents.

The internal inhibition and shyness was one of the major personal problem of girl respondents. Saraswathi and Radhika (1985) found the similar reasons causing low performance of girl students. Due to shyness and internal inhibition girls do not ask questions in class. Due to which their doubts are not cleared and they are unable to comprehend the subject matter adequately.

Lack of parental support and encouragement which the girl respondents perceived was another reason for their low performance. Gupta (1976) and Singh (1988) also obtained a close relationship between the parental behaviour, their support and encouragement they provide to their children and the performance of children in schools. This indicates that parents in rural areas are not interested to educate their girls or they feel the education as not important for girls. Moreover, parents themselves are not educated to help their children which is the prime demand of the present day education system. Since parents cannot meet this demand, the performance level of children specially girls remain low which ultimately pressurizes the girls to be out of the schools.

CONSTRAINT SCORES

The data in Table 4.13 reveal the constraint scores as obtained by the girl respondents have been discussed under following heads. The categories of constraints were made in the similar manner as adopted in case of constraints perceived by parents.

The opinion expressed by the respondents regarding constraints have been converted into scores following the procedure as adopted earlier while interpreting the perceived constraints of parents. Table 4.13 elucidates the distribution of scores as obtained by the respondents The constraints have been categorised as home constraints, school constraints, personal constraints and community constraints and finally all the four constraint scores have been pooled together and a composite score is obtained for overall interpretation of the constraint scores.

Home constraints: Table 4.13 shows that nearly three-fourth of the girls opined that home related situations pose mddium level of constraints in their education. Twenty one per cent respondents found home constraints as highly affecting their education and only 5 per cent respondents rated it in low level of constraints.

School constraints: More than half of the girl respondents i.e. 51 per cent reported school constraints as medium level and 46 per cent it as low level constraints. Only three per cent of the girl respondents perceived high level of home constraints in their education.

Personal constraints: In this case also girl respondents had perceived medium level of personal constraints while 44 per cent had perceived high level of constraints. Only 5 per cent of the girl respondents had perceived low level of personal constraints in their education.

Community constraints: More than three fourth (78%) of the girl respondents had perceived high level of commuuity constraints in their education. Whereas 21 per cent had perceived medium level of constraints and only one per cent had

TABLE 4.13

Distribution of girl respondents according to scores obtained on constraints perceived in education

(*N*=100)

S.No.	*Variable*	*Range*	*Frequency*
1.	*Home constraints*		
	Low	4-8	5
	Medium	9-13	74
	High	14 17	21
2.	*School constraints*		
	Low	19-24	46
	Medium	25-30	51
	High	31-35	3
3.	*Personal constraints*		
	Low	0-4	5
	Medium	5-9	51
	High	10-14	44
4.	*Community constraints*		
	Low	6-8	1
	Medium	9-11	21
	High	12-14	78
5.	*Composite constraint scores*		
	Low	45-56	48
	Medium	57-68	45
	High	69-80	7

Frequencies are in percentage as 'N' is 100

perceived low level of community constraints in their education.

Composite constraint scores: When all the scores are pooled together to obtain a composite picture of constraints we find that nearly half of the respondents i.e. 48 per cent had in general low level of constraints in their education. Forty five per cent had perceived constraints of medium levels and only seven per cent had perceived high level constraints.

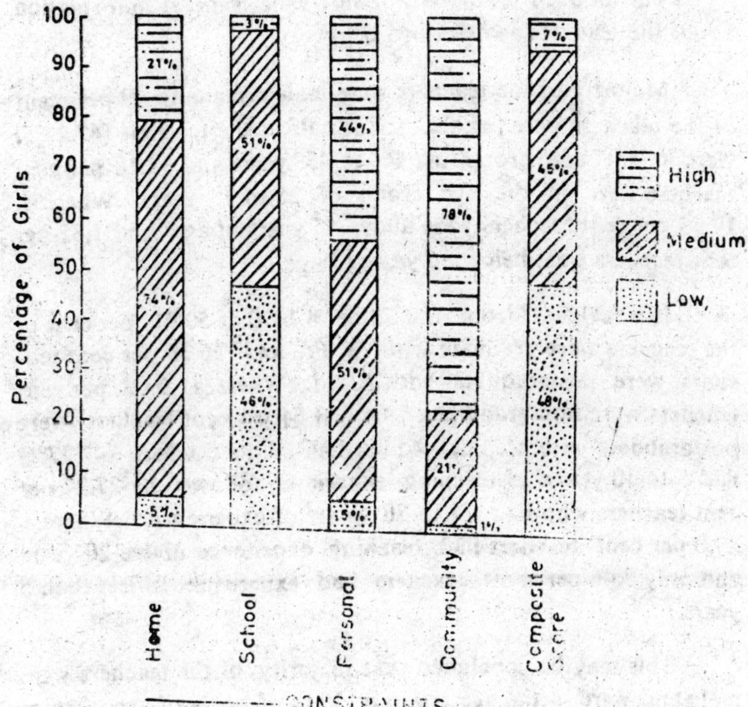

Fig. 4.6. Constraints Perceived by Girls in Their Education

It may be concluded from the data in Table 4.13 that majority of the respondents had high level of community constraints and medium level of home constraints. In case of personal constraints, almost equal number of respondents had medium and high level of constraints. While seeing the composite constraint scores it has been found that majority of respondents perceived constraints either medium or as low level.

TEACHER'S VIEW POINT

This section includes general information about the teachers, their attitude and constraints perceived in girls' education. The relevant information has been presented as under:

General information about the teachers

The data in Table 4.14 show the general information about the teachers as described below:

Majority of the teachers were male remaining 40 per cent of the teachers were female. About half of the teachers (47.27%) were in the age group of 36 to 45 years and 38.18 per cent teachers were in the age group of 25 to 35 years. Whereas, 17.73 per cent teachers were above 45 years of age and 1.82 per cent teachers were below 26 years of age.

It is evident from the Table 4.14 that 50.91 per cent of the teachers were graduate with B. Ed. and 36.36 per cent teachers were postgraduate with B. Ed. Whereas, 9.09 per cent teachers were non-graduates. Only 3.64 per cent teachers were postgraudate with M. Ed. About half of the teachers (47.27%) had 5 to 10 years of teaching experience followed by 27.27 per cent teachers who had 11 to 20 years of experience. Whereas 20.0 per cent teachers had teaching experience above 20 years and only 5.46 per cent teachers had experience of less than 5 years.

This may be concluded that majority of the teachers were male and were in the age group of 36 to 45 years of age. Majority of the teachers had qualification upto graduation along with the degree of B. Ed. and had five to ten years of teaching experience.

Teachers' attitude towards girls' education

The Table 4.15 shows the attitude of teachers towards the education of girls. The three categories that of unfavourable,

favourable and somewhat favourable have been made by dividing the total range into three equal categories as shown in Table 4.15.

Table 4.14
General information about the Teachers

(N=55)

Characteristics	*Category*	*Frequency*
Sex	Male	33 (60.00)
	Female	22 (40.00)
Age	Below 25 years	01 (01.82)
	25-35	21 (38.18)
	35-45	26 (47.27)
	Above 45	07 (12.73)
Qualification	non-graduate	05 (09.09)
	Graduate+B. Ed.	28 (50.21)
	Postgraduate+B. Ed.	20 (36.36)
	Postgraduate+M. Ed.	02 (03.64)
Experience	Below 5 years	03 (05.46)
	5-10	26 (47.27)
	11-20	15 (27.27)
	Above 20	11 (20.00)

Figures in parentheses denote frequency in percentage.

Table 4.15
Distribution of teachers according to their attitude toward girls' education

(N=55)

Attitude score (Range)		*f*	*percentage*
Unfavourable	(84-100)	1	1.82
Somewhat favourble	(101-117)	29	52.73
Favourable	(118-133)	25	45.45

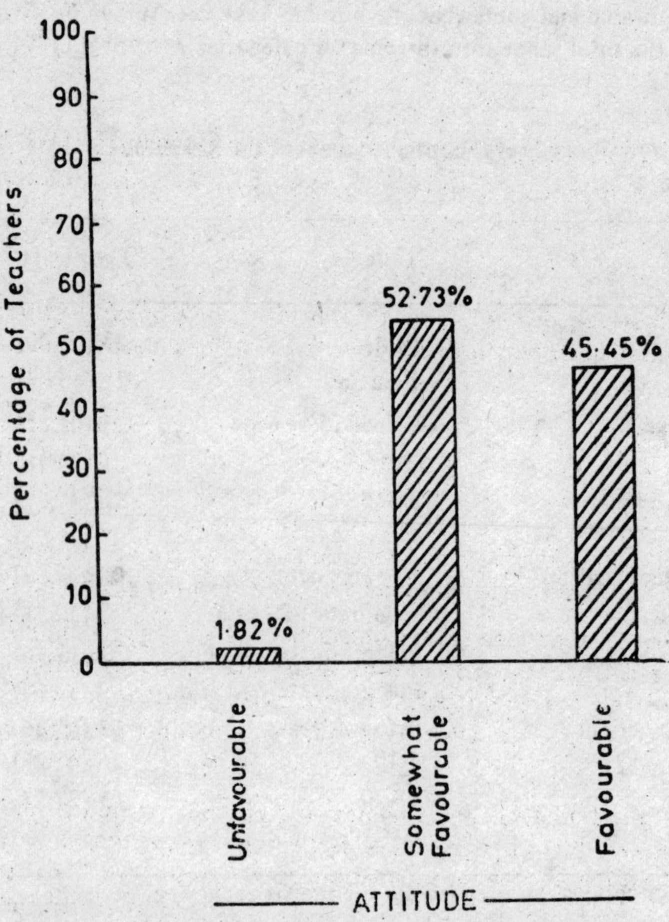

Fig. 4.7. Attitude of Teachers Towards girls' Education

It is evident that the majority of the teachers i.e. 52.73 per cent had somewhat favourable attitude followed by 45.45 per cent who had favourable attitude. Only a negligible number i.e. 1.82 per cent teachers had unfavourable attitude towards girls' education.

Thus, it appears that majority of the teachers had favourable or somewhat favourable attitude towards the education of girls. One teacher who had unfavourable attitude mainly stressed that under the present circumstances when income is limited, it is better to concentrate more on boys' education. Moreover, the nature of roles demanded from a girl are mainly home roles even after the marriage. Instead of investing the hard earned money on girls' education the same may be spent on the education of boys so that they can be on their own. The same teacher had the opinion that educated women are not better home keepers and their education is meaningless if they are not to take up any job. Moreover, she further stressed that it becomes difficut for the girls to go outside the village for their studies. Another problem of finding a suitable husband for a girl arises when she is educated. This teacher has stressed on the practical problems being faced under the present circumstances.

Constraints perceived by teachers

The relevant data have been presented as below:

Frequency of constraints perceived by teachers in education of girls

The data in Table 4.16 elucidate the following constraints:

Comprehension of the subject matter: Forty per cent of the teachers opined that it is rarely that girls are unable to understand the subject matter taught in the classes. There were 25.45 per cent teachers who never perceived poor comprehension in girls as a constriaint in their education. Whereas 34.55 per cent teachers found it occurring frequently that girls are unable to understand the subject matter.

Interest in studies: Majority of the teachers (49.09) did not find girls disinterested in studies. However, 29.09 per cent teachers found it occurring rarely. There were 21.82 per cent teachers frequently perceived this as a constraint in education of girls.

Regularity in home work: Twenty per cent of the teachers frequently perceived that girls do not do home work given to them and 36.36 per cent of the teachers also found this as a constraint but occurring rarely. However, 43.64 per cent teachers did not find it at all this as a constraint in education of the girls.

Table 4.16

Frequency distribution of teachers according to contraints perceived in education of girls

(N=55)

S.No.	Constraints	Frequency			Total
		FP	RP	NP	
1.	Lack of ability to understand the subject	19 (34.55)	22 (40.00)	14 (25.45)	55 (100)
2.	Lack of interest in studies	12 (21.82)	16 (29.09)	27 (49.09)	55 (100)
3.	Irregularity in home work	11 (20.00)	20 (36.36)	24 (43.64)	55 (100)
4.	Reaching school late	12 (21.82)	12 (21.82)	31 (56.36)	55 (100)
5.	Low attendance rate	14 (24.45)	09 (16.37)	32 (58.18)	55 (100)
6.	Shyness and hesitation in asking questions in classroom	21 (38.18)	22 (40.00)	12 (21.82)	55 (100)
7.	More discipline problems in co-educational schools	6 (10.91)	22 (40.00)	27 (49.09)	55 (100)
8.	Male teachers' inappropriate behaviour towards the girl students	6 (10.91)	10 (18.18)	39 (70.91)	55 (100)

(Contd.)

9.	Male teachers' hesitation in punishing girls even if they do not do home work	19 (34.55)	21 (38.18)	15 (27.27)	55 (100)
10.	Less number of girls in each class	34 (61.82)	7 (12.73)	14 (25.45)	55 (100)
11.	Parents' keeping their daughters busy in household work	31 (56.36)	17 (30.91)	7 (12.73)	55 (100)

Figures in parentheses denote frequency in percentage.

Punctuality: Nearly three fourth of the teachers i.e. 21.82 per cent opined that it is quite frequent that girls are not punctual in coming to school. The same number of teachers (21.82%) also perceived this as a constraint but occurring rarely while 56.36 per cent teachers did not perceive this as a constraint it all.

School attendance: Majority of teachers i.e. 58.18 per cent did not find that girls are not regular in coming to school and 16.37 per cent teachers rarely perceived this as a constraint. Only 25.45 per cent teachers frequently perceived this as constraint in education of girls.

Personality problem (Shyness and hesitation): It is evident that 38.18 per cent teachers frequently perceived and 40 per cent teachers rarely perceived that girls feel shyness and hesitation in asking questions in classroom. Whereas, 21.82 per cent teachers did not perceived shyness and hesitation among girls in asking questions in classroom.

Discipline problems in co-educational schools: About half of the teachers (49.09%) did not report the problem of discipline in co educational school as an obstacle in girls' education. However, 40 per cent teachers rarely perceived this as a constraint. There were 10.91 per cent teachers who frequently perceived this problem of discipline in co-educational schools as causing constraint in girls' education.

Male teachers' behaviour : Majority of the teachers (70 91%) did not report that male teachers do not behave properly with the girls. Whereas, 10.91 per cent of the teachers frequently perceive and 18.18 per cent of the teachers rarely perceived this as a constraint in education of girls.

Punishment problem : One third of the teachers (34.55%) frequently perceived that male teachers hesitate in giving punishment to girls if they do not do home work given to them. There were 38.18 per cent of the teachers who rarely perceived and 27.27 per cent of the teachers who did not perceive at all this as a constraint in education of girls.

Poor enrolement of girls : Majority of teachers (61.82%) frequently perceived that girls are less in number in each class affecting their group support and morale. Only 12.73 per cent of the teachers perceived this as a constraint but occurring rarely. However, 25.45 per cent did not perceive this as a constraint in educational of girls.

Household chores : More than half of the teachers (56.36%) frequently perceived that parents do not allow sufficient time to girls to study. Further, 30.91 per cent of the teachers perceived this as a constraint occurring rarely. Only 12.73 per cent of the teachers did not perceive this as a constraint in education of girls.

It may be concluded that major constraints perceived by teachers in education of girls were shyness and hesitation in asking questions in classroom, lesser number of girls in each class and parents keeping their daughters busy the whole day in household chores.

Shyness and hesitation was found one of the major problem of girls as perceived by teachers. Because of such hinderances the girls do not speak in the class. Their doubts are not cleared and they are unable to comprehend the subject matter. Similar reasons were reported by Saraswathi and Radhika (1985) for the low performance of the girls. This might be due to the reason that from very beginning girls are not allowed to participate in family discussions and later on it becomes their habit not to speak before those who are in position of any authority.

Teachers perceived another problem that of less number of girls in each class. Due to this there is difficulty in making groups of girls for their studies. The company is also needed for covering the distance between the school and home and also for enjoyment during free hours in schools. This strengthens not only the social ties but gives moral support to girls also. Bhandari (1982) also reported the similar findings causing low education among girls. Parental and community attitude, custom and their traditions might be the reasons for fewer girls attending schools.

As the parents and the girl respondents perceived the lack of time for studies due to household chores, the same reason was perceived by the teachers as causing low performance of the girls. Ojha (1966) and Bhaskaran (1989) also similar observations. It is the pressure of poverty of the rural parents that compel them to engage their children in labour to support their family income.

Constraint scores

The section of the chapter deals with the total scores on the constraints as perceived by the teachers in education of girls. These constraints have been shown as below in Table 4.17.

Table 4.17

Distribution of teachers according to scores obtained on constraints perceived in girls' education

(N=56)

Constraint range		*Frequency*	*Percentage*
Low constraint	(4-8)	19	34.55
Medium constraint	(9-13)	28	50.91
High constraint	(14-18)	8	14.54

The Table 4.17 shows that more than half of the teachers (50.91%) perceived the constraints in general as affecting girls' education moderately. There were 34.55 per cent teachers who perceived the constraints at low level. However, 14.54 per cent teachers perceived high level of constraints in education of girls.

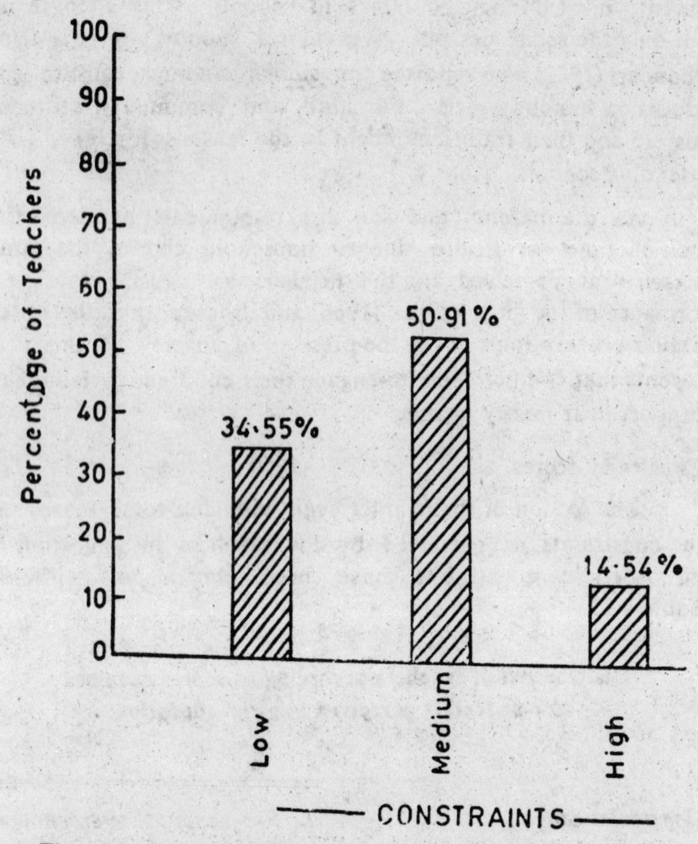

Fig. 4.8 Constraints Perceived by Teachers in Girls' Education

SCHOLASTIC ACHIEVEMENTS OF GIRL STUDENTS IN RELATION TO SOCIO-PERSONAL, ECONOMIC AND PSYCHOLOGICAL CHARACTERISTICS

The data related to socio-personal, economic and a few psychological characteristics have been presented in the following sections:

Association between family background variables and scholastic achievements of girls students

Under this section data have been presented under the following sub-heads :

Association between personal variables and scholastic achievements of girl students

Under this sub-head association between scholastic achievements of girl students and parents' age, education and ordinal position of the girls have been described as follows :

Parental age

Mother's age : Mother's age and scholastic achievements of their daughters have been shown in Table 4.18 as given below :

Table 4.18

Association between age of the mothers and scholastic achievements of their daughters

Mother's age	*Scholastic achievement*			*Total*
	Low (215-324)	*Average (325-389)*	*High (390-487)*	
Below 35 years	9	3	0	12
35-45 years	59	15	4	78
Above 45 years	16	1	3	10
Total	75	19	7	100

X^2 cal.=5.169 d.f. 4
X^2 tab.=9.488 Not significant
P is between 0.3 and 0.2

Table 4.18 shows that out of the 74 girls with low scholastic achievements, majority belonged to the mothers who were in the age group of 35-45 years. The frequencies in second column and third column also show similar results *i.e.* majority of average achievers and high achievers belonged to the mothers of the same age group. Thus, the table does not show any specific direction of relationship between these two variables, hence, chi-square is also non-significant.

Father's age : Father's age and scholastic achievements of their daughters have been shown in Table 4.19 as given below :

Table 4.19

Association between father's age and scholastic achievements of their daughters

Father's age	*Scholastic achievement*			*Total*
	Low (*215-324*)	*Average* (*325-389*)	*High* (*390-487*)	
Below 35 years	2	0	0	2
35-45 years	56	16	5	77
Above 45 years	16	3	2	21
Total	74	19	7	100

X^2 cal.=1.749 d.f. 4
X^2 tab.=9.488 Not significant
P is between 0.80 and 0.70

Table 4.19 shows that out of the 74 girls with low scholastic achievement majority belonged to the fathers who were in the age group of 35-45 years. The frequencies in second and third columns also show similar results *i.e.* majority of average achievers and high achievers belonged to the fathers who were in the same age group. Thus, the table does not reveal any specific direction of relationship between these two variables. Hence, the chi-square is not significant.

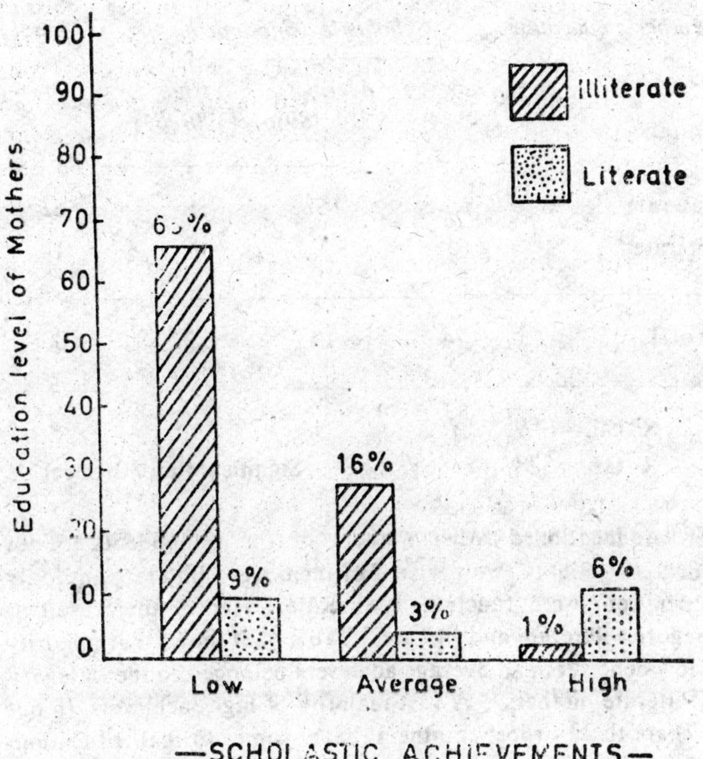

Fig. 4.9 Mothers' Education and Scholastic Achievement of their Daughters

Parental education

Mother's education : The education of the mothers and scholastic achievements of their daughters have been shown as below in Table 4.20.

Table 4.20

Association between education of the mothers and scholastic achievements of their daughters

Mother's education	*Scholastic achievement*			*Total*
	Low (215-324)	*Average (325-389)*	*High (390-487)*	
Illiterate	65	16	1	82
Literate	9	3	6	18
Total	74	19	7	100

X^2 cal. = 17.99* d.f. 2
X tab. = 5.99 Significant at 0.01 level

As mentioned earlier mothers of the respondents are not educated. Eighty-two per cent of them were illiterate and only 18 per cent were functionally literate. Hence, there are two categories-illiterate and literate. Table 4.20 shows that majority of low acheivers and average achievers belonged to the category of illiterate mothers. A vast majority of high achievers (6 out of 7) are those whose mothers have some formal education. Chi-square results also show significant relationship between these two variables. Thus, it can be said that mothers' literacy has positive impact on girls' scholastic achievement. It means when the mothers are literate, the scholastic achievement of their daughters is high and when mothers are illiterate, the scholastic achievements of their daughters is low.

Father's education : The education of the fathers and scholastic achievements of their daughters have been shown as below in Table 4.21.

Table 4.21

Association between father's education and scholastic achievements of the girl students

Father's education	*Scholastic achievement*			*Total*
	Low (215-324)	*Average (325-389)*	*High (390-487)*	
Illiterate	23	7	0	30
Upto Matriculation	48	8	3	59
Above Matriculation	3	4	4	11
Total	74	19	7	100

X^2 cal. = 15.06* d.f. 4 Significant at 0.01 level
X^2 tab. = 9.48

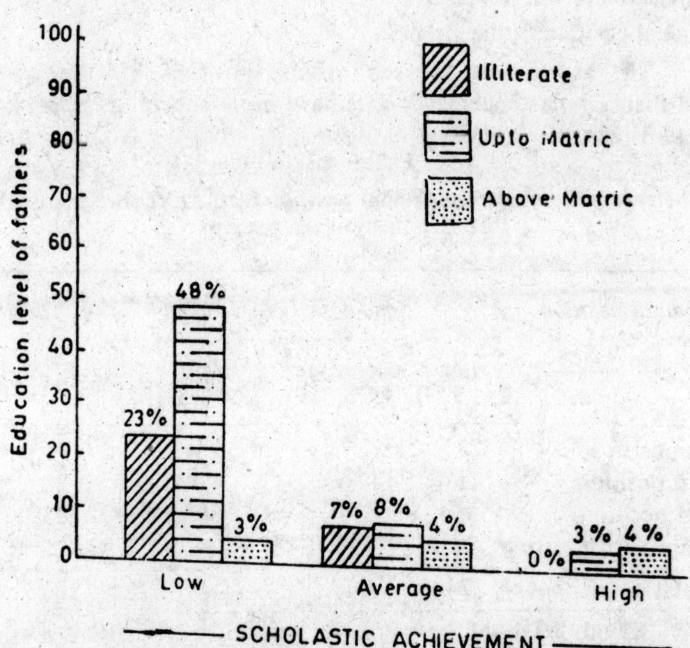

Fig. 4.10 Fathers' Education and Scholastic Achievement of their Daughters.

In case of fathers' education also three categories *viz.*, illiterate, upto matriculation and above matriculation were formed after merging the primary and middle with the category of upto matriculation and the graduates with the category of above matriculation. Table 4.21 shows that about of 74 girls with low achievement, majority belonged to fathers who have education upto matriculation and those who are illiterate. The frequencies in second column also show the same that majority of average achievers also belonged to the same categories. But out of 7 girls with high achievement, majority belonged to fathers who were with education above matriculation or upto matriculation. Chi-square results also show significant relationship between these two variables. Thus, it can be inferred that father's literacy also has positive impact on girls' scholastic achievement. It can be said that when the level of education of fathers increases the scholastic achievement of their daughters increases and vice-versa.

Ordinal position of the girls

The association between ordinal position of the girls and their scholastic achievements have been shown as below in Table 4.22.

Table 4.22

The association between ordinal position of the girl students and their scholastic achievements

Ordinal position	*Scholastic achievement*			*Total*
	Low (215-324)	*Average (325-389)*	*High (390-487)*	
Ist position	25	7	0	32
2nd position	15	4	1	20
3rd position	16	4	3	23
Above 3rd position	18	4	3	25
Total	74	19	7	100

X^2 cal. 2.218 d.f 6

X^2 tab. 12.59 Not significant

P is between 0.90 and 0.80

Table 4.22 shows that out of 74 girls with low achievement, majority were first born in the family. The data is second column also show that the majority of average achievers were first born. But out of seven girls with high achievement majority belonged to the category of third ordinal position and above third original position. This shows that there is some relationship between ordinal position and the scholastic achievements of girls. Since the chi-square calculated was not significant there is no observable definite impact of girls' ordinal position on their scholastic achievements.

FIG. 4·11. FAMILY SIZE AND SCHOLASTIC ACHIEVEMENT OF GIRLS

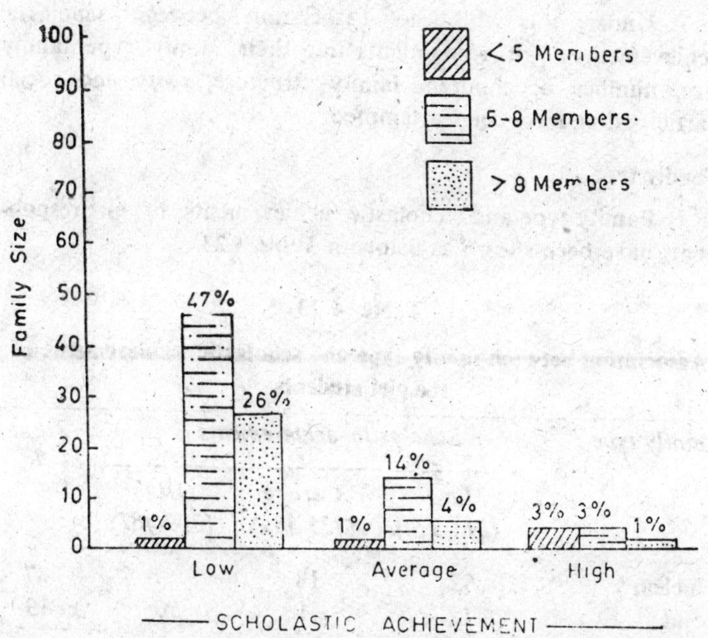

Out of the personal factors affecting scholastic achievements of girl students, the study revealed that parental age and ordinal position of the girl respondents were not found significantly associated with their scholastic achievements. But the parental education (both mother and father education) was found significantly associated with the scholastic achievements of the girl respondents. This finds the support of Medsker (1963), Plowden's (1967), Mathur and Hundal (1972), Rajguru *et al.* (1975), Sharma (1982) and Contractor (1984). These authors too found that education of the parents is associated with the scholastic achievements of their children. This might be due to the reason that educated parents could teach and guide their children while the uneducated could not teach and guide their children. Uneducated parents might not support and encourage the education of girls.

Association between social variables and scholastic achievements of the girl students

Under this sub-head association between scholastic achievements of girl respondents and their family type, family size, number of children, family structure, caste and social participation have been attempted.

Family type

Family type and scholastic achievements of girl respondents have been shown as below in Table 4.23.

Table 4.23

Association between family type and scholastic achievements of the girl students

Family type	*Scholastic achievements*			*Total*
	Low (215-324)	*Average (325-389)*	*High (390-487)*	
Nuclear	62	18	7	87
Joint	12	1	0	13
Total	74	19	7	100

X^2 cal. = 1.097 d.f. 2
X^2 tab. = 5.99 Not significant
P is between 0.50 and 0.70

Table 4.23 reveals that out of 74 girls with low achievement, majority belonged to nuclear family. The frequencies in columns second and third show that majority of average and high achievers also belonged to nuclear family only. Chi-square calculated was found not significant. Hence, it can be inferred that family type has no impact on the scholastic achievements of the girl students.

Family size

The association between family size and scholastic achievements of girl students have been shown below in Table 4.24.

Table 4.24

Association between family size and scholastic achievements of the girl students

Family size	*Scholastic achievement*			*Total*
	Low (*215-324*)	*Average* (*325-389*)	*High* (*390-487*)	
< 5 members	1	1	3	5
5—8 members	47	14	3	64
> 8 members	26	4	1	31
Total	74	19	7	100

X^2 cal.=13.5* d.f. 4

X^2 tab.=9.488 Significant at 0.01 level

Table 4.24 shows that out of 74 girls with the low achievement, majority belonged to the families with the size of five to eight members and more than eight members. Table further shows that second column also show similar results *i.e.*, majority of average achievers belonged to the same families only, But out of 7 girls with high achievement majority belonged to families with less than five members and five to eight members. Chi-square calculated was found significant. Hence, it can be said that family size has its impact on scholastic achievements of girls. The girls belonging to small or moderate size families are high achievers and belonging to large family size are low achievers.

FIG. 4·12. NUMBER OF CHILDREN IN THE FAMILY AND SCHOLASTIC ACHIEVEMENT OF GIRLS

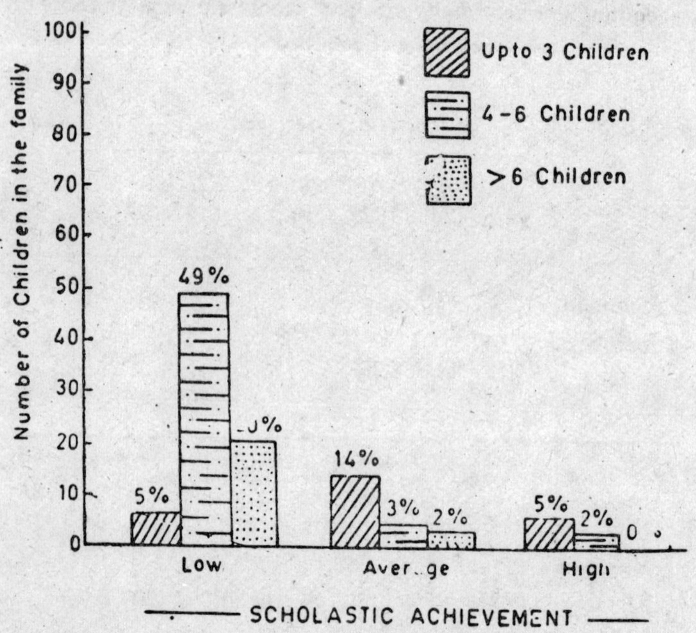

Number of children in the family

Number of children in the family and scholastic achievements of girls have been shown as below in Table 4.25.

Table 4.25

Association between number of children in the family and scholastic achievements of girl students

Number of children	*Scholastic achievement*			*Total*
	Low (215-324)	*Average (325-389)*	*High (390-487)*	
Upto 3	5	14	5	24
4—6	49	3	2	54
6	20	2	0	22
Total	74	19	7	100

X^2 cal.=39.05* d.f 4

X^2 tab.=9.488 Significant at 0.01 level

The data of the Table 4.25 show that out of 74 girls with low achievement, majority belonged to the families with four to six number of children. Whereas, majority of the average achievers and high achievers belonged to the families having children not more than three. The chi-square calculated was found to be significant. Thus, it can be inferred that number of children in the family have their impact on the scholastic achievements of the girl students. Where there are more number of children in the family the achievement level of girls was low and where there were less number of children in the family, achievement level of children was comparatively high.

Family Structure

Structure of family and the scholastic achievements of girls have been shown as below in Table 4.26.

Table 4.26

Association between family structure and scholastic achievements of girls students

Family structure	*Scholastic achievement*			*Total*
	Low (215-324)	*Average (325-389)*	*High (390-487)*	
Only girls	1	0	0	1
Girls with one boy	8	5	2	15
Girls with boys	48	11	5	64
One girl with boys	16	3	0	19
Cnly one girl	1	0	0	1
Total	74	19	7	100

X^2 cal. $=6.526$ d.f. 6

X^2 tab. $=12.59$ Not significant

P is between 0.5 and 0.3

Table 4.26 shows that out of 74 girls with low achievement majority belonged to families having girls and boys and the families having one girl with several boys. But out of 19 average achievers and 7 high achievers majority belonged to families who were having several girls with several boys and families having several girls with one boy. But, the chi-square value was found not significant. Hence, it can be said that family structure had no impact on the scholastic achievements of girls.

Caste

Association between caste and scholastic achievements of girl students have been shown in Table 4.27.

Table 4.27

Association between caste and scholastic achievements of the girl students

Caste	*Scholastic achievement*			*Total*
	Low (*215-324*	*Average* (*325-389*)	*High* (*390-487*)	
Lower	9	1	0	10
Middle	28	3	2	33
Higher	37	15	5	57
Total	74	19	7	100

X^2 cal. =3.814 d.f. 4

X^2 tab. =9.488 Not significant

P is between 0.40 and 0.30

The data in Table 4.27 reveal that out of 74 girls with low achievement, majority belonged to higher caste. The frequencies in column second and third show that majority of average achievers and high achievers also belonged to higher castes only. Chi-square calculated was found to be not significant. Hence, it can be inferred that caste has no impact on the scholastic achievements of the girl students. The high achievers and low achievers are distributed almost similarly among three caste categories i.e. low, middle and higher.

Social participation

Social participation and scholastic achievements of girl students have been shown in Table 4.28.

Table 4.28 shows that out of 74 girls with low achievement, majority belonged to the fathers who were not the member of any formal organization. In case of average achievers and high achievers also majority belonged to fathers who were not member of any formal organization. Thus, results do not show any specific direction of relationship between these two variables. Hence, chi-square was found not significant. So, it can be inferred that social participation of fathers had no impact on scholastic achievements of their daughters.

Table 4.28

Association between social participation and scholastic achievements of girl students

Social participation	*Scholastic achievement*			*Total*
	Low (215-324)	*Average (325-389)*	*High (390-487)*	
Not member of any organisation	67	18	5	90
Member of one organisation	7	1	2	10
Total	74	19	7	100

X^2 cal. = 1.111 d.f. 2
X^2 tab. = 5.99 Not significant
P is between 0.70 and 0.50

Among the social factors affecting scholastic achievements of the students, the type of family, family structure, caste and social participation were not found significantly associated with the scholastic achievements of the girl respondents. However, the size of family and number of children in the family were found significantly associated with the scholastic achievements of girl respondents. Similar findings were also reported by Mathur and Hundal (1972), Zajone (1976) and Mani (1980) who found that size of family affect the scholastic achievements of children. As regards number of children in the family, Contractor (1984) obtained number children in the family affecting the scholastic achievement of the children. This might be due to the over crowding in the family that disturbs the children specially the girls whose attention is diverted towards the domestic work. This also happens due to the unsupporting comments from various members of the family. Their presence may also be disturbing and destracting the attention from studies and attracting towards what they talk and discuss about. Elder or younger all members of family expect girls to work for them.

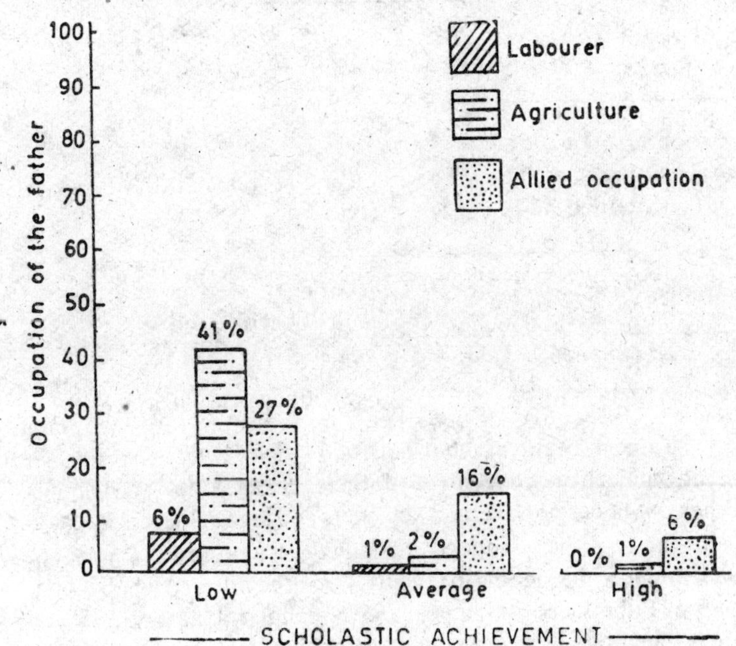

Fig. 4.13. Occupation of the Father and Scholastic Achievement of Their Daughters.

Association between economic variables and the scholastic achievements of the girl students

Under this sub head association between scholastic achievements of the girl students and occupation, annual income and land owned by the family have been discusssed below:

Occupation of the Father

Association between occupation of the fathers and scholastic achievements of their daughters have been shown in Table 4.29.

Table 4.29

Association between occupation of the fathers and scholastic achievements of their daughters

Occupation	*Scholastic achievement*			*Total*
	Low (215-324)	*Avarage (325-389)*	*High (390-487)*	
Labourer	6	1	0	7
Agriculture	14	2	1	44
Allied occupation	27	16	6	49
Total	74	19	7	100

X^2 cal.$=$14.50* d.f. 4

X^2 tab.$=$9.488 Significant at 0.01 level

Table 4.29 shows that out of 74 girls with low achievement, majority belonged to fathers engaged in agriculture. Whereas, in case of average achievers and high achievers majority belonged to fathers engaged in allied occupations. Chi-square was found to be significant. Thus, it can be inferred that occupation of fathers had its impact on the scholastic achievements of their daughters. Hence, girls belonging to fathers engaged in agriculture and labourship could not get time for studies. Moreover, because of parents being uneducated they could not help in studies. While others having fathers in service could have availed this advantage.

Annual income and scholastic achievement of the girl students

Association between annual income of the family and scholastic achievements of the students have been shown in Table 4.30.

Table 4.30

Association between annual income of the Family and scholastic achievements to girl Students

Annual income	*Scholastic achievement*			*Total*
	Low (*215-324*)	*Average* (*325-389*)	*High* (*390-487*)	
<Rs. 10,000	10	1	0	11
Rs. 10,000-35,000	36	12	2	50
>Rs. 25,000	28	6	5	39

X^2 cal. = 2.554 d.f. 4

X^2 tab. = 9.488 Not significant

P is between 0.70 and 0.50

Table 4.30 shows that out of 74 girls with low achievement, majority belonged to families having annual income of Rs. 10,000 to Rs. 25,000. In case of average achievers also majority belonged to the families with annual income of Rs. 10,000 to Rs. 25,000. But in case of high achievers majority beloned to families with annual income of above Rs. 25,000. Hence, there appears some association between these two variables. Since chi-square was found not significant, it can be inferred that income of the family has no significant impact on scholastic achievements of the girls. Girls whether from rich family or poor family suffer almost equally because of social and other factors rather than economic ones.

Land owned by the Family

Land owned by the family is another indicator of economic status of the family. The distribution of the land owned by the members of the families of respondents have been shown in Table 4.31.

Table 4.31

Association between land owned by the Family and scholastic achievements of girl students

Land owned	*Scholastic achievement*			*Total*
	Low (215-324)	*Average (325-389)*	*High (390-487)*	
No land	11	4	0	15
<5 acres	12	8	1	28
6-20 acres	28	3	6	37
>20 acres	16	4	0	20
Total	74	19	7	100

X_2 cal.=7.73 d.f. 6

X^2 tab.=12.59 Not significant

P is between 0.3 and 0.20

The data in Table 4.31 show that out of 74 girls with low achievement, majority belonged to families having 6 to 20 acres of land. But in case of average achievers, majority belonged to families having less than five acres of land. In case of high achievers, majority belonged to the families with 6 to 20 acres of land. Chi-square calculated was not significant. Thus, it can be inferred that land owned by the family has no impact on the scholastic achievements of the girls.

Under economic factors affecting scholastic achievements of girl students, annual income of the family and land owned by the family have not been found significantly associated with scholastic achievements of the girl respondents. But occupation of the father has been found significantly associated with their daughters' achievements. The similar findings were observed by Medsker (1963), Plowden (1967), Singh (1969) and Sinha (1973). This might be due to the reason that in occupations like agriculture and labourship parents are unable to give attention to studies of their children and along with this, their children have to support their parents in their agriculture and labour work. On the other hand, those who are in service are educated to some level and moreover, have limited working hours. The off time in the evening or morning, they can spend with their children guiding in their studies.

Scholastic achievements of the girl students in relation to socio-economic status and some psychological characteristics

The correlation between the scores of scholastic achievements of girl students and the scores on their socio-economic status and some psychological characteristics have been attempted in order to find out the extent of relationship between the variables. The same has been presented in Table 4.32.

Correlates of scholastic achievement of girl students as presented in Table 4.32 reveal that scholastic achievements of girl students was significantly and positively correlated with perental socio-economic status. However, the extent of correlation was low. This shows that SES of the family affects girls' scholastic achievements to some extent only. The positive correlation shows that higher the SES, higher is the level of scholastic achievement. The same has been supported by Chopra (1969), Dhami (1974), Srivastava *et al.* (1975), Kundu (1977), Siddique *et al.* (1983) and Deepika (1990). The positive correlation might be due to the fact that parents with better socio-economic status could provide better facilities for the education of their girls whereas, others might not have done it.

The Table 4.32 also reveals that achievement motivation of the girl respondents had positive and significant but low correlation with their scholastic achievements. The similar results were obtained by Mehta (1969), Parikh (1978), Tandani (1984) and Singh (1991). The positive correlation shows that if students have higher level of achievement motivation their performance level will also be high. Thus, if there is high achievement motive then the students will strive and work hard to achieve the higher level of performance in examination. They may surpass the obstacles.

Table 4.32

Correlation between scholastic achievements and socio-economic status and some psychological characteristics

Variable	*'r' values*	*Level of extent*
Socio-economic status of parents	0.23+	Low
Girls' Psychological Characteristics		
Achievement motivation	0.21+	Low
Goal Discrepancy score (Level of aspiration)	0.07	Not Significant
Attainment Discrepancy score (Level of aspiration)	—0.05	-do-
Number of times goal reach score (Level of aspiration)	—0.07	-do-
Academic anxiety	—0.28+	Low
Constraints in education perceived by girl respondents		
Home constraints	—0.31+	Low
Personal constraints	—0.85+	High
School constraints	—0.62+	Substantial
Social constraints	—0.62+	do-
Composite constraint score	– 0.84+	High
Parental Psychological Characteristics		
Attitude towards girls' education	—0.56+	Substantial
Perceived constraints in education by parents		
Home constraints	—0.49+	Substantial
Personal constraints	—0.75+	High
Social constraints	—0.75+	-do-
Composite constraint score	—0.94+	-do-

+Significant at 0.05 level of probability

Attitude of the parents was also found significantly correlated with the scholastic achievements of the respondents. The direction of correlation was positive and the extent of correlation was substantial. Thus, if parents have high positive attitude towards girls education, this helps girls in raising their academic performance. The similar findings have been reported by Mehra (1977), Bose (1978), Sinha (1983), Shah and Nagia (1984), Saraswathi and Radhika (1985) and Singh (1988). The correlation between attitude of parents and scholastic achievements of their daughters show that the girls with parents having positive attitude towards their education get a good deal of encouragement and support from their parents for education whereas, others are devoid of the positive attitude of parents which affect their success and progress in education.

The academic anxiety among students was found to have significantly negative but correlation with the saholastic achievements of the girl students was low. The results show that the anxiety lowers the performance of the girls. Such findings have been reported by Goblin and Singh (1974), Kirpal Kaur (1976), Soman (1977) and Nair (1988). The negative correlation might be due to the reason that students with anxiety could not do better in examinations. As a result, they could not reach the maximum level of their potentials. On the contrary, the girls with low anxiety could do better in absence of any type of fear or tension arising out of the anxiety.

Table 4.32 further shows that the level of aspiration of students was not found significantly associated with their scholastic achievemehts. This shows that if girls aspire high, it does not help them in raising their performance level. The similar results have been reported by Muthayya (1962), Camerson (1977) and Madho (1977). The results indicates that there are other important factors than the aspiration level which affect the scholastic achievements of the students. The correlation between scholastic achievement and the home constraints as perceived by girl students and their parents was negative. It was statistically significant, however, the extent was substantial and direction negative. This shows that if the constraints are more, the performance will be low. On the other hand, those students will perform higher who have faced less home constraints. The similar findings have been obtained by Joseph (1973), Ismail (1975), Muralidharan (1980) and Bhaskaran (1989). Due to the home constraints, students could not engage themselves in the studies which resulted in their lower performance.

Personal constraints of girls were found significantly correlated with their performance. The coefficient of correlation is high and negative in direction. The results indicate that the students who have perceived higher level of personal constraints like lack of interest in studies have performed poor in their examinations. The students who lack interest in studies search execuses for not giving sittings for studies. This will adversely affect their performance in examinations. Similar findings were given by Skiera (1990) that mainly the low interest of the students in studies causes low performance.

School constraints as perceived by girl students were found statistically significant. The coefficient of correlation is negative and substantial. Due to poor facilities in schools the performance of the students was adversely affected. This finds the support of Daniel (1976), Gupta (1976). Saleh (1985) and Shah (1991).

Community constraints as perceived by parents and girl respondents were also found significantly correlated with the scholastic achievements of the girl students. The correlation is high but negative in direction. This might be due to community customs, traditions and general opinion and attitude which are affecting the education of girls. Thus, the composite constraints or constraints in general as perceived by parents and their daughters were found high but negative which was statistically significant. The similar results were given by Pillai (1975), Bhandari (1982) and Talesra (1986).

Multiple regression analysis of independent variables

Multiple regression analysis of only those independent variables for which the correlation was found significant has been presented in the Table 4.33.

Table 4.33

Multiple regression analysis of significant independent variables

Independent variables	*b values*	*t values*	*Rank*	R^2	*F value*
Socio-econmic status	0.50	2.47+	III		
Girls' Psychological Characteristics					
Achievement motivation	0.73	2.28+	V		
Academic anxiety	0.23	0.29	IX	87.74	47.34+
Constraints in education					
Home constraints	6.65	2.27+	VI		
Personal constraints	—3.80	—1.00	III		
School constraints	—0.83	−0.27	X		
Community constraints	—9.18	−3.91+	I		
Composite constraint score	5.22	1.85	VIII		
Parents' psychological characteristics					
Attitude towards girls' education	0.80	2.45+	IV		
Constraints in education					
Home constraints	4.58	3.07+	II		
Personal constraint	0.00	0.00			
Community constraint	0.00	0.00			
Composite constraint score	0.00	0.00			

+Significant at 0.05 level of probability.

It is evident from the Table 4.33 that thirteen selected variables were responsible for 87.74 per cent of variation in the scholastic achievements of the girl students. The F value 47.34 (13.88 d.f.) was highly significant. Thus, out of the thirteen variables, six of them *viz.*, socio-economic status, achievement motivation of the girl students, home constraints and community constraints as perceived by girl respondents in their education, attitude of parents towards girls' education and home constraints perceived by parents in girls' education were able to account for the maximum variation in the scholastic achievements of girls.

Hence, it can be said that these above mentioned six variables are most important factors in increasing or decreasing the scholastic achievements of girl students.

Teacher's attitude and perceived constraints in girls' education

The relevant data have been presented under the following two heads :

Teacher's attitude

The rank correlation between the scholastic achievements of girl students of a school and attitude of teachers of that school has been shown in Table 4.34.

Table 4.34 elucidates that the students of GHS Matarsham obtained the highest marks hence, obtained highest rank in scholastic achievements of the girl students. Other schools in order of their ranks were GHS Talwandi Rooka, GHS Hindwan, GHS Chirod, GHS Shahpur, GHS Juglan, GHS Satrod Kalan, GHS Neoli Kalan, GHS Arya Nagar, GHS Kirtan and GHS Bhagana.

The ranks assigned to schools on the basis of attitude scores of the school teachers of these schools were somewhat similar to the ranks obtained by the schools on the basis of achievements of students. The calculated value of rank correlation was found to be significant (P=0.65) at 0.05 level of significance. This implies that the ranks given on the basis of average scholastic achievements of the schools and the attitude of teachers towards giris' education of that schools

Table 4.34

Correlation between scholastic achievement and attitude of teachers

S No	School	Average marks	Attitude scores	Rank R_1	Rank R_2	Diff. [D]	D^2_7
1.	Matarsham	357	131	1	1	—	—
2.	Talwandi Rooka	329	121	2	3	1	1
3.	Hindwan	315	118	3	4	1	1
4.	Chirod	309	117	4	5	1	1
5.	Shahpur	300	129	5	2	3	9
6.	Juglan	299	111	6	10	4	16
7.	Satrod Kalan	297	108	7	11	4	16
8.	Neoli Kalan	296	115	8	8	—	—
9.	Arya Nagar	284	112	9	9	—	—
10.	Kirtan	280	116	10	6.5	3.5	12.25
11.	Bhagana	268	116	11	6.6	4.5	20.25
							76.50

Rank correlation P=0.652+

+Significant at 0.05 level of probability.

were in agreement. This indicates that teachers' attitude is positivelty and significantly correlated with the scholastic achievements of the girl students.

The similar results were reported by Routray (1988) that teachers' involvement and attitude affect the scholastic achievement of the students.

Constraints perceived by teachers

The rank correlation between the scholastic achievements of girl students and constraints perceived by their teachers in girls' education has been shown in Table 4.35.

It is evident from the Table 4.35 that the girl students of GHS Matarsham obtained highest marks and obtained highest rank in scholastic achievements of girl students. Other

Table 4.35
Correlation between scholastic achievement and teachers' perceived constraints in girls' education

S. No.	*School*	*Scholastic achievement*	*Cons-traints*	*Rank* R_1	R_2	*Diff.* $\|D\|$	D^2
1.	Matarsham	357	9	1	7.5	6.5	42.25
2.	Talwandi Rooka	329	6	2	11	9	81.00
3.	Hindwan	315	8	3	9	6	36.00
4.	Chirod	309	7	4	10	6	36.00
5.	Shahpur	300	10	5	5	—	—
6.	Juglan	299	13	6	2	4	16.00
7.	Satrod Kalan	297	11	7	3	4	16.00
8.	Neoli Kalan	296	9	8	7.5	0.5	0.25
9.	Arya Nagar	284	14	9	1	8	64.00
10.	Kirtan	280	10	10	5	5	25.00
11.	Bhagana	268	10	11	5	6	36.00
							Σ = 352.50

Rank correlation P= – 0.603+

+Significant at 0.05 level of probability

schools in order of their ranks were GHS Salwani Rooka, GHS Shahpur, GHS Juglan, GHS Satrod Kalan, GHS Neoli Kalan, GHS Arya Nagar, GHS Kirtan and GHS Bhagana.

The rank assigned to schools on the basis of the constraints perceived by the teachers of that schools were more or less in opposite direction. Hence, the correlation value is high but negative (P= – 0.60). The value of coefficient of correlation is statistically significant at 3.05 level. This implies that the level of scholastic achievements of the students of different schools and the constraints perceived by the teachers of those schools in the education of girls were negatively correlated. When teachers perceive more constraints this may affect their towards girl students and as a result, girls' performance is also affected. The ultimate effect is on girls' school results.

The similar results were obtained by Rai (1975), Shukla (1983) and Saraswathi and Radhika (1985) that the constraints which the teachers perceive in girls' education affect the scholastic achievements of girl students.

STRATEGY FOR ENHANCING THE SCHOLASTIC ACHIEVEMENTS OF GIRL STUDENTS

A strategy is a complete and detailed plan of work to be conducted with a mission to benefit the disadvantaged. This includes the skills values, art of manoeuvring the campaign or other programmes. Thus, strategy needs to be planned stressing on the programmes, methods, materials and skills. A strategy is being planned based on the results of the study, for enhancing the level of the study, for enhancing the level of scholastic achievement of girls living in rural areas.

The educational problems of girls in our country is of vital importance. However, more important is the issue of girls' education and that specially in rural areas which necessitate special programmes and a special strategy for implementation of the programmes because of special problems being faced by them.

The results obtained from the study discussed so far have highlighted the status of rural girls' scholastic achievement and the problems perceived by the persons who are directly involved in the process and emergent need is to draw plan for systematic implementation of the programme so that hinderances can be minimized so as to let way for enhancement of scholastic achievement of rural girls.

Under this section, the strategy for implementation of programme runs through various phases. First the problems are summed up and then remedial measures are suggested.

Finally all are combined to draw up one programme including the means and processes to achieve the goals.

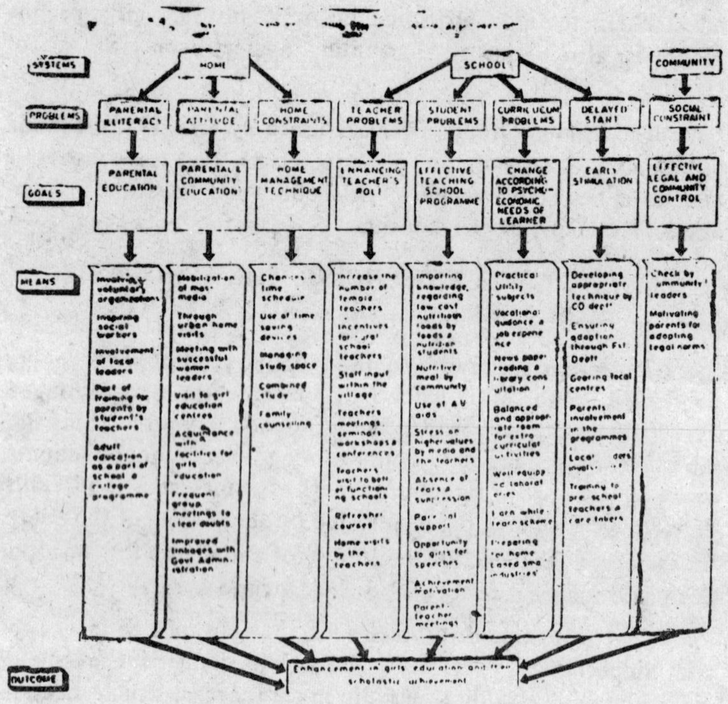

Fig. 4.14. Strategy for Enhancing the Scholastic achievement of Rural Girls.

HOME RELATED PROBLEMS

Parental Illiteracy

Parental illiteracy has emerged as one of the important negative force. The illiterate parents can neither realise the importance of education nor, they appreciate their children spending time on various educational activities. Moreover, they are unable to guide or help their children in the learning process. This problem can be solved by increasing the literacy among parents and involving those people or agencies in guiding children who are educated themselves and can help in the process. Thus, parents and students both need assistance.

Parental literacy can be enhanced through adult literacy programmes which should be mobilised in true spirits. The coordination between various voluntary and Government organisations and agencies would give fruitful results. The national social services like NSS and NCC can be given this responsibility of teaching adults. The volunteers of Nehru Yuva Kendras can also be involved. Some new clubs of enthusiastic youth can be established for the purpose of teaching adults. The adult literacy programme can further be strengthened by making it an essential part of various degrees. The student-teachers of training institutions and other students of agricultural universities and other educational institutions should be entrusted with a job of teachin grural people. This can be made an essential requirement of their degrees.

Generally the rural people are over-burdened with their occupational jobs. Due to economic pressures, men and women both work from morning till evening. They are generally tired in the evening and then a number of other domestic and social obligatory jobs are waiting for them. They may not spare time for attending regular classes. As per their needs the volunteers are to be sent to their residential places and to their places where they work. At residential places, the classes should be held in the evening as per their suitability. Such centres are to be conducted near to their residential places. If possible, home visits should be preferred to motivate them, to teach them and to prepare them for developing positive attitude towards their daughters' education. If programme will be very attractive and very useful for them, this will motivate them to squeeze some time from other work and spend on education.

During the teaching sessions some psychological aspects of human nature should also be kept in mind. The attractive material should be used, they should be motivated properly showing their long range benefits. Teachers should have enough patience, their attitude towards learners' should necessarily be positive. They should not hurt by criticising them rather the sense of human respect for learners, helpful attitude towards learners are the essentlal requirements of the 'teachers'. There are number of new techniques being developed as some time seen on television also, those can be used for making their teaching programme interesting and effective. To use the psychological principles of learning and retaining, it will be very fruitful, if teaching is done by using the material or material symbol which those people know well and those articles are in their daily use. For example, for teaching the Hindi letter 'न' the word 'Nalka' can be used as the shape of Nalka and the Hindi letter with which it starts resemble very much.

This learning-teaching process should be made enjoyable and not any burden on anyone. If paid workers are deployed, it may be just a formality whereas, if the work is entrusted to those people who work with spirit of dedication and social service may be fruitful. The bond between learner and teacher is stronger and dissemination of knowledge becomes easier. Hence, it is suggested that voluntary organisations, social workers should be mobilised for such cause.

The traditional people of our villages still have faith in their leaders and they obey or follow them. Thus, it will accelerate the speed by economizing the time and effort, if local leaders are involved in motivating the people for education.

Parental Attitude

The unfavourable attitude of parents towards girls' education is the by-product of illiteracy handed down to them to generation after generation. The unfavourable attitude towards girls' education, thus, has been rooted firmly in our socio-cultural mileu. Such strong and deep rooted thoughts and feelings are hard to change. Though, the need is to change the attitude of parents and the community as a whole. If the first goal of parental literacy is achieved, this goal of changing parental attitude will be achieved easily. Attitudes are not changed so easily, hence, multiple techniques should be used for change. Popularizing alone through mass-media will not be much effective in bringing out the change in actual practices. Though these days, there is a lot of stress on girls' education in the advertisements or other programmes being telecast on television. But the question who uses it and how it is interpreted remains unanswered till there is face to face contact with those people. The mass-media or other media of publicity can create interest only if the messages reach upto them. The adoption process does not stop here because there are number of difficulties in acceptance of the message and application of the practices which the respondent needs to be satisfied. Hence, besides mass-media publicity, other methods should also be stressed. It is suggested that meetings can be arranged in the villages by involving the local leaders and other influential people. In such meetings various doubts and inhibitions raised by the people should be cleared. Those people also need to be convinced regarding the short range and long range benefits to be gained through acceptance of the changed practices. The gains are to be counted in terms of economic and social benefits.

A change in parental attitude can further be strengthened by arranging visits to the families whose daughters are well educated, settled and managing vocational and home roles efficiently. When they themselves will see the educated girls' changed status, they will be convinced more. They can also be brought to cities and see the educational institutions where girls are studying and acquiring skills in various jobs. Their visits to urban families can further motivate them for the change in favour of girls' education. The Government is granting a number of facilities for the education of girls which many rural people do not know. There is also need to improve the linkage between the rural people and the government administration. Frequent visits of officers involved in the developmental processes along with the group of ladies will help in motivating them for sending girls for education.

Both cultural differences and sex differences in achievement have been found to result from parents' differential expectations, values and emphasis on achievement. Parental expectations for boys and girls differ and are reflected in their attainments. In a study of mathematical achievement (Parsons *et. al.*, 1982), it was found that children's attainment values were related to the value, parents assigned to different areas of achievement. Parents considered mathematics more important for sons than for daughters. Moreover, in spite of the fact that boys and girls performed equally well in school, parents had lower expectation of success for daughters than for sons. In addition, both boys' and girls' expectancies of success were more highly correlated with their parents' expectations for them than with their own past performance (Hill, 1980).

Parents' beliefs influence children's perceptions of their own abilities, their attitudes towards various areas of achievement and their expectations for success and failure. These lead to emotional responses, ways of labelling themselves and situations, attributional styles and strategies in tackling cognitive tasks that directly affect the children's cognitive performance and achievement.

In addition to parental expectations, a supportive warm home environment that encourages exploration, curiosity and self-reliance leads to high achievement (Kelly and Worell, 1977), In malevolent homes characterized by extreme punitiveness and rejection, or in homes where the father is extremely authoritarian and enmishes the child in rigid rules and regulations, low achievement results (Bradley *et. al.*, 1977 and Radin, 1976). Such restrictiveness may inhibit early exploration and curiosity in children. It also seems probable that such parental behaviours lead to insecurity and high anxiety in children, factors that play an increasingly salient role in interferring with intellectual performance and academic achievement over the school years (Ferguson, 1970). Finally, family interactions where parents make responses contingent on childrens' behaviour contribute to the sense of mastery and self efficiency that underlies successful problem solving and achievement.

There is some evidence that interactions between sex of the parent and sex of the child must be considered in evaluating other parental influences on cognition. Some of the findings sugguest that although mothers may be more important in stimulating intellectual development and achievement needs in both boys and girls, fathers may have relatively more influence on cognitive growth in daughters than in sons (Hathrington and Parke, 1986).

It may be that because children spend more time with their mothers than with their fathers in our culture, the mother is most important in determining the intellectual level of the home environment. Mothers also seem to be more important than fathers in shaping the aptitudes of their children. When university students had fathers who were less educated than their mothers, their aptitude scores were higher than those of students whose fathers were the better educated parents. This occurred inspite of the fact that homes with the more educated fathers were of higher socio-economic status. Variations in the mothers' education seem to counteract the commonly found effect of social class factors on children's aptitudes (Willerman and Stanfort, 1972). Thus, it is suggested that mothers as well as fathers be included in the training programmes for inculcating the right attitudes and habits for stimulating the child's mental abilities in early years. The package for early stimulation including parents should be developed, tested and properly applied. For this purpose, the focal centres like Anganwadis be selected and home visitors may be entrusted with the job. Mass-media geared in popularizing the package and some popular local leaders can be associated in the programme who will visit the families and schools as well.

Home Constraints

Lack of time due to involvement of children in various household jobs has emerged as one of the important home constraints. Due to poverty the rural parents involve their children in various household chores as well as they involve their children in family occupations to supplement the family income. The results obtained with regard to the impact of social and economic status of the family on educational attainment of the rural girls also show that the girls from low socio-economic status obtain lower achievement on scholastic tests and vice-versa. As regards the social status, it is the caste which determine the child's performance in schools. Caste may not be directly related but there are number of other factors associated with the caste which directly affect the child's performance in school. In Indian social structure the social power, the political power and the economic power have remained with the dominant castes. Those who are rich, are progressive also and have better social contacts, better exposure to emerging social needs. They have better access to facilities and opportunities. It has been seen that the upper caste people though uneducated themselves sent their daughters for education in best institutions of the country. This happens because they know the value of education and also because they could afford the expenditure. Since, these people know more about the worth of girls' education, provide every facility to their daughters for education.

The economic status of the family which the generally goes side by side with the social status, fuvours the girls' education. Since they have enough money, they have access to various media, viz. radio, television, newspapers, magazines and their mobility is also more than other people. Their visits to other places including metropolitan and other cities enable them to adopt new values and so is the case with girls' education. Sending girls in good institutions, meeting expenditure on private tuitions, providing various types of books, stationery and other required material is easier for these people. Hence, the girls' education in upper socio-economic status gets facilitated. Some other family members also happen to be somehow educated, they support directly and indirectly also by boosting up the morale and creating educational environment in the family. The child gets stimulated for learning right from the beginning.

The children of low socio-economic status suffer more and specially the girls because of negative attitude of parents and their own society, lack of financial resources and girls' requirement in the family to help in various ways. She takes care of younger ones, cooks food and performs otner household jobs to spare the parents for earning. Hence, her attention is diverted, time is smashed in addition to the fact that resources are limited. Family environment is neither supportive nor stimulating. Accepting these limitations the need is to draw a programme suitable to them. We need a system which demands lesser time in schools, give less home work and subjects taught to them are based on utility. Some earn-while-learn programmes can be strengthened. Parents of such students need more motivation in their own terms based on their needs. Though goverument has various programmes, under which students specially girls of poor families get financial benefits in the form of scholarship, stationery, books and dress/uniform. The authorities should take responsibility of disbursing the same to those who need or for whom it is meant. The social recognition to the donors will motivate many new people who offer scholarship or other financial assistance to these girls. Parents normally take it granted that their children if educated will surely get job. But, we know that it may not be possible. But if girls' education is such that it prepares the girls for independent earning, it will be a very strong motivating force for the parents. Girls need to be taught and trained in various skills like tailoring, knitting, embroidery, food processing, food preservation, animal husbandry, etc., so that they can earn on their own.

If girls can be prepared mentally to take up some home based small industries, the mission of girls' education will be appreciated more by all sectors. The school timings should not clash with their parents' timings. These little modifications or extra financial strain on government involved can do a lot in improving the situation.

Various economic problems are related to ignorance, illiteracy and adhering to values which have led to delay in adoption of small family norms. Large family has resulted further into degrading economic conditions. Similarly, family conflicts or unhealthy family relations have also been observed related to socio-economic status. Study of children in such families is adversely affected because of uncongenial and non-conducive environment for their education. Increasing awareness about the necessity of limited family size and motivating them for acceptance of measures for controlling the family size are to be taken up through various media. Strategy for this purpose should be based on through understanding of human psychology which stresses upon arousal of need, readiness for accepting change, readiness for self direction, satisfaction of other emerging secondary social needs etc.

It has been reported invariably that lack of time and lack of parental attention to children and lack of physical facilities in homes have affected the education conversely. Though, parents, being busy with their occupational and home activities is beyond our control, however, some measures can be popularized which save their time in cooking, water, fuel and grain storage. The time saving devices like improved smokeless chulhas, solar cookers, pressure cookers and many other technues can be popularized. It is also suggested that school timings can be adjusted to the needs of such girls who help their parents in various household activities. Starting classes in early hours in the morning may not suit to them, hence, it can be adjusted as per their convenience. The school curriculum may also teach the boys to help the parents and their sisters by sharing the responsibilities with them. Atleast they can be made self-sufficient by doing their own work by themselves.

As regards physical constraints students have pointed out the need of proper light facilities and secluded place, which is required for creating calm and quiet atmosphere conducive for learning. Though, we know that it cannot be provided in small houses and providing separate room is almost out of questions in those houses. However, some place can be searched out where children of close vicinity, can sit together and carry on their study. The back courtyard, front varanda or same place under the tree can be covered to give the feeling of separate study area. Though, this does not require much expenditure and can be done with minimum alterations, the only need is to make the parents and community aware of this need.

Some mothers can be prepared to stimulate the child's learning ability even while doing cooking and other household jobs. Even fathers can be taught to make best use of their time.

some effective time management activities have to be evolved and popularized. For grownups, the illiterate parents cannot guide, for which special learning classes in the village are suggested where children of different classes sit together and help each other. Thus, the child to child support programmes can prove effective in this regard.

SCHOOL RELATED CONSTRAINTS

Teacher problems

Teacher, students and curriculum are the three main components of school institution. Each one is important and needs to be given proper attention. As regards teachers, it has been observed that respondents prefer and feel comfortable sitting in a class when a teacher is female. Though, in lower classes there are number of female teachers but in higher classes say in high school the number of female teachers is less as compared to male teachers specially in rural areas. Such problems have their own various socio-cultural origins. The national planners can pay attention to such issues.

Generally, it has been observed that there is reluctance on the part of teachers to serve in rural areas. In order to create and maintain their interest in this noble profession some incentives like rural allowances, free and proper accommodation, transportation allowances should be provided. Staff input can be from within the village. Another aspect of teachers behaviour which have been found important is their interest in teaching and the child. Their behaviour towards the child and unhealthy sobial relations within themselves are some of the problems experienced by the respondents. Alongwith these, teachers' punctuality, attitude and their calibre affect their pupils to a great extent. Such issues are vital and should be taken care of properly. If some seminars, workshops, refresher courses and short term trainings are arranged for creating awareness, awakening, inspiration and support to teacher, which can help in bringing about the change in positive direction. Such teachers' interaction with the better and dedicated teachers can be encouraged by arranging their visits to better schools and places. Teachers' behaviour can be checked by the controlling authorities regularly.

The home task should be assigned to the students regularly and checked thoroughly by the teacher concerned only. The teacher should avoid partiality among the students and they should not rely on monitors. Teachers must take extra care of those students who are poor in studies. Bhasin (1985) reported that teachers who accept pupils' feelings, praise them, use their perceptions and involve them in the teaching-learning transaction enable them to improve their academic performance better than pupils whose teachers by virtue of their patience and understanding influence pupils, perception positively. Most of the pupils in such teachers' classes were close to their capacities. Teacher-taught-parent ties needs to be strengthened and the easiest would be if teachers pay visits to the families of the students. Their interaction will bring them closer to each other and to the child also.

Students' problems

As the health of the student is of great importance, the teachers must keep a check on health of the students. Medicines should be provided to the students if they are ill. If there is major illness then parents must be informed and assisted in availing the doctor's help. To get better scholastic achievement in the school better or nutritious food intake is also needed which the poor parents cannot afford. Hence, atleast one time meal in the school should be provided to the students by the community itself. The students of Foods and Nutrition department in Home Science college should suggest low cost nutritious foods. The students belonging to Extension Education department can popularise these foods in the villages.

Interest among students for studies must be developed by using various audio-visual aids, healthy competition must be encouraged among students. The habit of cheating in examinations must be controlled by supervision and vigilance. Students' interest in studies should be developed through appropriate means.

Many teachers have reported that the girls remain submissive in classes. They hesitate and do not ask questions for clarity. If some questions are asked to them, they reply with much hesitation. In fact this acts as a barrier in the process of learning. Teachers should encourage the girls to speak in class. The punitive practices or authoritarian personality of the teachers do not permit the girl students to be bold in the classrooms. The problem begins in early school age where teaching is done through fear. The root of the problem might be in parental practices of suppression and discrimination between the girls and boys. Parents and teachers, both have to encourage the girls by teaching the appropriate way of self-expression in family as well as in school. The in-built inhibitions are to be removed from the very beginning years of girls' development. The deep foundations of inequality of the sexes which is built in the minds of men and women during the process of socialization is further strengthened by peer groups, schools, neighbourhood and the media. This gender based discrimination is to be removed from all walks of social life, if girls are to be educated in true spirits.

Motivation, anxiety and fear have been found related to the academic achievement of the students. McClelland *et al.* (1955) indicated that achievement motivation is developed in the early relationship between a child and his parents. In the early few years of his life, if the growing child receive a good amount of recognition, praise and reward for his accomplishments, he develops the feeling of personal worth, some sense of recognition and some sense of achievement. It is important for the development of achievement motivation that the child is exposed to a high standard of excellence and is encouraged for his performance and independent efforts. Achievement motivation is an overall tendency to evaluate one's performance against standards of excellence and to strive for successful performance (Feld *et al.*, 1979). Achievement motivation varies among children and for the same child across tasks, situations and times.

Variations in achievement motivation and performance are often related to emotions and opinions about certain learning tasks and may be convinced of their inability to learn in certain areas. Mathematics is particularly a troublesome area for some people, especially females. Negative emotions can serve as a block to effective learning by directing a considerable amout of cognitive effort to make anxiety producing, self defeating self evaluation. "I am going to fail, again"; "I cannot do this"; "I cannot pass multiple choice exams", such negative thoughts distract the learner from the details of the task and can have an immobilizing effect on learning (Brown *et al.*, 1983). Children with learned helplessness are unlikely to increase their efforts and to apply new strategies in the face of difficult problems since they believe that the causes for their failure are beyond their control (Deweck and Elliot, 1983).

The motivational level should be increased through building spirit of healthy competition, setting higher goals but within their reach and encouraging them to achieve the goal. Parental practices that engender emotional security and low anxiety, independence, and high internalized goals for achievement are associated with accelerated cognitive development. Parents who value achievement and set high achievement standards, have children who have high achievement motivation and make more sustained efforts to attain their goals (Crandall *et al.*, 1969; Rosen and D'Andrade, 1959).

Anxiety and fear must not have hinderance in the studies of the students. Teachers should provide environment for studies which is free from anxiety and any type of fear regarding examination results and future career. Parents and other family members should also motivate and encourage the students for good performance in the examinations. Home enviornment should not cause any type of anxiety, fear, nervousness and other health problems among the students. As children go through the early elementary school years they become more able to set realistic standards of achievement. In the same period anxiety about academic achievement and failure on tests accelerates. It may be that children's introduction to the competitive atmosphere of the classrooms, where children are tested graded, evaluated and tracked, contributes both to the increased use of social comparison and to increased test anxiety (Ruble *et al.*, 1980 ; Parsons, 1982).

In a programme developed by Feuerstein (1980) which involves prompting to help children improve their problem-solving strategies but also is oriented toward altering the child's general relations to the task and the situation. By putting himself in the role of a helper rather than a tester, the teacher-therapist helped to reduce the child's anxiety. Another ploy used by such interventionists is to focus on the difficulty of the material rather than the ability of the child to learn it.

Many schools arrange parent-teacher meetings with a purpose to increase understanding between the two important sources of child's learning of various habits and acquisition of knowledge. If such meetings are held regularly, can play an important role in inspiring the child for education and solving various problems. By involving parents more and more in the process, the difficulty arising out of non-supportive attitude can be solved.

Curriculum problems

The curriculum problems have been found as an important hinderance in the achievement of the respondents. The curriculum should be adapted to the needs of the people. The course curriculum should be modified and made easy to suit the psycho-economic needs and cultural framework of the society. The approach should be of making it of practical utility in the real life situation. The educational system should be re-oriented to make it job oriented. The vocational training should be started in elementary classes itself so that their interest in building career for opting a vocation is sustained. Course work must be planned in an interesting way by the teachers. The teaching method must involve use of some type of audio-visual aids, field trips, visits to other educational and vocational training centres so that the interest in learning is maintained and motivation for career is developed.

Studies have shown that girls find difficulty in comprehension of mathematics and science subjects. Whereas, they perform better on language and other Arts subjects. Keeping this in mind, teachers can use some different methods making science and mathematics easier. More time should be spent on these subjects. Teachers should repeat the difficult subjects. More practical exercises must be given with regular checking of the answers. Teachers must assign home work to students regularly and must check the very next day so that students may develop a habit of doing studies every day. Teachers get the feedback on effectiveness of their teachings through examinations which should be conducted very frequently. Extra curricular activities have their own role in the school programme. This increases students' interest in school and learning also. This makes the school experiences pleasant ones. Students' participation in curricular and extra-curricular activities should be encouraged and proper recognition and rewards must be given.

The interest in studies can further be increased by inculcating the habits of newspaper reading and utilizing library facilities. There should be stress on practical learning. The laboratory should be well-equipped and subjects should be taught through learning by doing not only learning by learning and seeing. Rao (1976) found that the more global approach to the environmental correlates of achievement is the teaching conditions in a school. He found that the school-teacher-pupil variable is a great predictor of achievement of children. Of course, separately the school, teacher and pupil vairable show correlation with achievement but their combined predictive value is much high. Thus, it seems that an attempt to improve school academic performance through a combined approach will be more fruitful than these variables in isolation.

Early stimulation

It is a universally accepted truth that child's development begins from very early years of life. Some reports have supported that the process of development begins right from the birth. The home environment, the interaction level, the information input and processing all help the infant to grow and develop his potentialities to optimum level. Hence, it will be of immense value if, such techniques are developed and popularized among the parents to adopt for stimulating the mental abilities of the child. Some scientific researches are pinpointing the behaviour to be stimulated for development in early stages and also the specific techniques to be applied for stimulating the development. However, a more thorough work is needed in our country before giving the final shape to the programmes for extensive use by the people.

After home, the responsibility shifts ro pre-schools. The pre-school programmes have done excellent job in stimulating the child's mental abilities. The ICDS programme has done good job in establishing the Anganwadi centres in rural and urban slum areas. In Haryana state, there are 92 blocks out of 108 blocks where ICDS programme is in operation. This covers 80 per cent of the population in the state. There are total 9,863 Anganwadi centres catering to the needs of seven lakh children. However, the functioning of these centres can be made more effective by implementing the intervention programmes for accelerating the mental growth of the child. Many studies have reported the gains in later school performance of the children who have had attended pre-school programmes.

Results obtained from similar compensatory programmes also provided considerable encouragement. Some studies have shown that while teaching the disadvantaged by using tangible rewards and punishments during language and other subject drills, it had produced substantial IQ gains in the children.

It is also suggested to try a model in which children are engaged in activity for the sake of pleasure of the activity rather than to obtain reward or to avoid punishment. It has been reported by some authors that there is more gain to IQ when intervention programmes introduced in 3 year old than the gain in 4 year olds. This suggests that the intervention programmes should be adopted as early as possible and should work using the psychological laws and principles of learning.

Pre-school intervention programmes such as, Head Start two or three years after termination of the projects when the children were in their early elementary school years, the children seemed to be showing little sustained academic advantage resulting from the intervention. However, in contrast to the results of short-term follow up studies of children who were involved in pre-school intervention projects in the 1960's indicates that there may be positive but delayed, effects of intervention (Lazar and Darlington, 1982).

The investigators compared their results to those of other major pre-shool intervention programmes and concluded, "Programmes that have many hours and years of contact with the families and particularly many hours of direct contact with the children, are likely to have the most positive effect on children's intellectual outcomes" Ramey *et al.*, 1985).

The effects of intervention programmes are not restricted to the target child. In one programme involving both mother and child in a pre-school centre, one-third of the mothers subsequently enrolled in school to finish their school work (Miller, 1967). The experience of actively participating in their child's education and of feeling responsible for initiating changes in the child may help develop a sense of competence and initiative in the mother that partially mitigates the feelings of helplessness and of being eternally controlled that are frequently found in lower class people.

The effects also extend to young siblings of the children receiving the enrichment programme. Young siblings of the children involved in such activities show test performance superior to that of children in homes where the older child is not in an enrichment programmes (Klaus and Gray, 1968).

Intervention programmes are not only for poor. In few studies in which middle class children were included, these children and their mothers also benefitted from the experience of early intervention. One investigator comments, "Middle class children respond beautifully ... most of them literally soar in it" (Caldwell, 1973).

In Indian situation, Anganwadis are playing an important role in early stimulation of children. But it has been seen through many surveys that if there is only one or two Anganwadis in a village, all parents do not send their children which is either due to distance, or lack of interest on the part of the parents. In a survey, it has been observed that the attendance of children is more at the time of food distribution but remains thin during the rest of the time. Anganwadis in fact did not have variety of programmes to generate interest in children and women (Kanta, 1991).

Problem can be solved if number of Anganwadis are opened in nearly places. Volunteers and social workers can be encouraged to take up responsibility of this noble job. Hence, it is suggested that these Anganwadis should be started on the basis of community cooperatives where extension workers and teachers in need of training, can also join the staff at such centres. In this way, early stimulation programmes can be encouraged for extensive utility.

There is every need that each child should be attended individually. All children are alike, each child has special needs. The infant respond selectively to the stimulation in the environment They seem to show fairly consistent preferences for certain kinds of stimulation at different ages. Infant with special problems do not show these preferences as clearly and may not benefit from training in this area. Any stimulation programme must take the individual differences of the infants into consideration, with particular care on the way these individual differences with regard to the infants reactivity to stimulation and the kinds of response the infant initiates from the environment. Every child enters school with a unique background and thus, starts out with a different body of knowledge and set of understanding. Concern with these variations in children's congnitive development has resulted in increased attention to early childhood education. It has become now important to introduce the basic concepts in pre-school and primary grade curricula like it is taught in early intervention programmes. Since basic concepts are both foundamental to understanding verbal instruction and essential for early school achievement.

The teacher often needs to identify and remediate weaknesses in basic concept comprehension, particularly at the time of school entrance. Teachers should realize that the same concepts are easier for some children and difficult for other student groups, and mastery often takes place at varying rates. For example, basic concepts present particular difficulty for learntng disabled children and other special need groups. Researches indicate that pupils who start out behind tend to stay behind and also that the gap between good and poor achievers tends to become wider and wider over time. The effects of basic concepts' deficiencies may be cumulative, the greater attention should be devoted to correct initial lags in concept mastery and language development. Lags in many cases have been traced to pre-school deprivation in such learning experiences (Boehm, 1986).

Thus, it is suggested that the early educational programmes should be very comprehensive and may include the following components: (i) to improve the physical health and abilities of the child; (ii) to help improve the emotional and social develeopment by encouraging their self confidence, spontaneity, curiosity and self discipline; (iii) to improve mental processes and skills by paying attention to conceptional and verbal skills; (iv) to establish patterns and expectations of success; (v) to increase the child's capacity to relate positively to family members and other people; (vi) to strengthen the family's ability to ralate positively to children and their problemst (vii) to develop a responsible attitude towards society on the part of the child as well as towards family; (viii) to foster constructive opportunities for society to work cooperatively with the poor in solving problems and (ix) to increase the child's and the family's sense of dignity and self worth.

SOCIAL CONSTRAINTS

There are number of other constraints in the education of girls which are social in nature. The major social constraints that have emerged during the study are a few strong social evils. Out of those, important ones are early marriage and social security of the girls. Probably both are related to each other. The insecurity has led to the custom of early marriages. More number of children in the family is another cause of early marriage. Viewing the interrelatedness of various social problems, a comprehensive programme must be chalked out. The messages for small family, medical facilities, appropriate age of marriage and benefits of girls' education, all should be combined in one message. The legal aspects of such practices should also be popularized. They are playing good role in this regard. But their reach upto the rural poors, must be ensured. For creating awareness, the need is to start door to door campaign and also the people's movement. The community and the community leaders must be involved in the process in motivating parents for sending their girls for education and not marrying the girls before the prescribed age. Some useful training in income generating activities may encourage the parents to send their girls to schools. As regards security, again the job should be entrusted to the community itself. The government, the volunteers, parents and the teachers must take inittative in solving the problem of girls' security. The need is to motivate both parents and the students not to marry while they are studying. The teachers and other volunteers can educate people in this regard.

In the last, it is suggested that a more comprehensive, need-based educational programmes for girls should be planned throughly involving the specialists from various fields fields like Education, Psychology, Child Development and Extension disciplines. This programme should be started in a village which will act as a 'Model Village' and also the source of inspiration for others. The community leaders, parents and social welfare organizations should also be involved in programme. The tested model can further be extended to other villages with modifications.

5

Summary and Conclusion

Education is the process through a continuous reconstruction of experiences. It is the development of all those capacities in the individual which enable him to control his environment and fulfil his responsibilities in more effective manner. Education can play a decisive part in making women aware of their aspirations, their real potential and their rights. On viewing the history of educational development, we find that women constitute the larger proportion of illiterates. Besides founding the proper schooling of girls, it is although more important to see that they perform well and also they continue to study further. Scholastic success serve as the foundation for further studies as well as a source of inspiration for higher achievements. Scholastic achievement in case of girls is much important because their further studies depend largely upon the level of their achievements.

There are number of factors that affect the scholastic achievements of the girls. The socio-economic status of the parents, lack of time, psychological environment at home family relations of the child, educational facilities, etc. Besides, these, social class, education and social opportunities also set important limits on their attainments.

To find out the root cause of low achievement and to suggest remedial measures to curb the problem, the present study was undertaken with the following objectives:

1. To find out the scholastic achievements of the rural high school girls
2. To assess the factors affecting scholastic achievements of the girl students
3. To suggest a strategy for enhancing the scholastic achievemens of the girls.

The study was conducted in a cluster of eleven villages of Hisar district having girl students in tenth class selected randomly. Respondents included 100 girl students studying in class tenth from the eleven villages, their respective parents and 55 teachers of the students.

Scholastic achievement was the dependent variable for the present study. The personal, social, economic and psychological characteristics were the independent variables. The personal, social and economic characteristics included the age and education of parents, ordinal position of girls, type and size of family, number of children in the family, family structure, caste, social participation, occupation, annual income and land owned by the family and socio-economic status of parents. The psychological characteristics included the achievement motivation, academic anxiety and level of aspiration of girl students, constraints perceived by the girl respondents, parents and teachers in the girls' education and also attitude towards girls' education.

An interview schedule was specifically developed for the purpose. Frequency, percentage, chi-square, correlation, multiple regression and rank correlation were used for the analysis of the data.

The following results were obtained:

1. Majority of the respondent girls (74%) were low achievers who got third division, 19 per cent were average achievers who got second division and 7 per cent were high achievers who got first division. There was no girl student with merit. Hence, it can concluded that girls' achievement was low.

2. Majority of the girl students got third division in subjects *viz.*, Hindi, English, Mathematics, Science and Social Studies

followed by second divisioners in the same subjects. There was no student with merit in science and social studies, whereas, negligible number i.e. only 1 student got merit in Hindi and 2 got merit in English. But there were 12 per cent who failed in science and 11 per cent in social studies. However no student failed in Hindi. This means science and social studies were difficult for girl students but Hindi was easiest subject for them.

3. Drop out rate was higher after eighth grade as compared to after ninth level. The important reasons for drop outs were marriage and excess load of household work. Failure rate was also higher at eighth level.

4. Majority of the mothers and fathers were between the age group of 35 to 45 years. Majority of the mothers were illiterate while majority of the fathers were educated upto matric with almost equal number of illiterates.

5. Majority belonged to nuclear family with five to eight number of members in the family. Majority of the families had four to six number of children who were both boys and girls. Majority belonged to higher caste whose fathers were never a member of any organization.

6. Majority of the fathers were engaged in agriculture having annual income of Rs. 10,000 to 25,000. Land owned by majority of the families was five to twenty acres and they belonged to low socio-economic status.

7. The major home constraints perceived by parents in girls' education were lack of family assistance in teaching and guiding, lack of separate space for study, lack of time and lack of interest in educating girls.

8. The major personal constraint of girls perceived by parents was lack of interest of girls in studies.

9. The major community or social constraints perceived by parents were early marriage of girls, more importance given to home/field work, less number of girls having attended schools and feeling of guilt by girls while not assisting parents in their

work. In general, major constraints were community constraints and personal constrains of girls affecting their education.

10. Majority of the parents were having unfavourable and somewhat favourable attitude towards girls' education.

11. There were almost equal number of girls having first, second, third and above third ordinal position.

12. Majority of the students were having high achievement motive but majority were moderately anxious. Aspiration level of the students was also not much high.

13. The major home constraints perceived by girls in their education were lack of family assistance in teaching and guiding, lack of time, lack of positive attitude of parents and lack of separate place to study at home.

14. The major school constraints perceived by girl students were lack of library facility, lack of lay teachers, difficulty in proper grasp of the subject matter, non-interesting presentation of material in books and indiscipline caused by boys.

15. The main personal problems were internal inhibition while asking questions in class room and lack of parental support and encouragement.

16. The major community constraints as perceived by girls were importance given to home/field work, community disapproval of a girl sitting and studying while parents are working, early marriage of girls and less number of girls having attended school. The major constraints for girls were community constraints and home constraints.

17. Female and male teacher ratio was 4 : 6. Majority of the teachers were in the age group of 25 to 45 years, who were graduates and postgraduates with B.Ed. Majority possessed five to ten years of experience in teaching.

18. Almost equal number of teachers possessed somewhat favourable and favourable attitude towards girls' education.

19. The major constraints perceived by teachers in girls' education were less number of girls in the class and parents not giving time to their daughters for studies. So, the constraints were not much for the teachers.

20. Mother age, father age, ordinal position of girls, family type, family structure, caste, social participation, annual income and land owned by the family were not found significantly associated with the scholastic achievements of girl students. But education of mother, education of father, size of family, number of children in the family and occupation were found significantly associated with the scholastic achievements of girl students.

21. Socio-economic status, achievement motivation and attitude of parents towards girls' education were positively and significantly correlated with the scholastic achievements of girls while academic anxiety in girls, their home, school, personal, community and composite or general constraints and the home, personal, community and general constraints perceived by parents in girls' education were found negatively and significantly correlated with the girls' scholastic achievements.

22. The thirteen selected variables which were found significantly correlated with the scholastic achievements of girls were responsible for 87.74 per cent variation in the scholastic achievements of girls. The factors which were able to account for maximum variation were socio-economic status, achievement motivation of the girls. Home and community constraints perceived by girls in their education, attitude of parents towards girls' education and home constraints perceived by parents in girls' education.

23. Attitude of teachers towards girls' education and the constraints perceived by teachers in girls' education were also found significantly correlated with the scholastic achievements of girl students.

24. As regards strategy for enhancing the scholastic achievement of the rural girls, various problems were identified based upon the perception of rural girls, their parents and theri

teachers. Goals have to be achieved through various means by involving different agencies like community leaders, parents and social welfare organizations. The programme should be started in a village which will act as a 'Model Village'. The tested model can further be extended to other villages with modifications.

Suggested areas for further research

A results of the study have perported some areas for future research which are given here under :

1. A study can be conducted on the factors which are not included in the present investigation, but may be important like the self concept. emotional maturity, intelligence, home/school adjustment, etc., in relation to scholastic achievement of the students.

2. The study can be conducted on a large area and the composite solutions can be advanced on the basis of results.

3. A study can be conducted to practize the planned strategy in some villages and effects may be evaluated for further improvement.

4. A comparative study of factors associated with the scholastic achievement of boys and girls can be conducted.

Bibliography

Abrahason, S. 1952. Schcol rewards and social class status. Educational Research Bulletin, 31 : 8-15.

Aggarwal, S. 1978. Relationship of academic achievement to intelligence and family relations. Unpub. M.Sc. Thesis, P.U., Chandigarh.

Ahluwalia, S.P. and Shyam, D. 1975. A study of relationship between socio-economic status and academic achievement of high school students. Journal of Educational Research and Extension. 12(1) : 5.

Ahuja, C. 1973. Continuing education in India—A plan for action. The Education Quarterly. 14(1): 28.

Annamalai, K. and Venkata Subramanian, P. 1972. Case study of a few students who have secured high marks in SSLC examinations. Indian Psychological Abstracts. 1(1) : 59.

Atkinson, J.W. and Litwin, G.H. 1960. Achievement motivation and test anxiety concerned as motive to approach success and motive to avoid failure. Journal of Abnormal and Social Psychology. 2 : 52-63.

Bartlett and Smith, L.P. 1966. The influence of testing conditions on need for achievement scores and their relationship to performance scores. In Atkinson, J.W. and Feather, N.T. A Theory of Achievement Motivation. John Wiley and Sons, New York, pp. 277-297.

Bhandari, R.K. 1982. Educational development of women. Education Quarterly. 34(3) : 12-14.

Bhangoo, S.R. and Lakshmi Anand. 1975. A comparative study of achievement motivation of the rural and urban boys in Punjab. Indian Journal of Home Science. 9(1) : 19.

Bhargava, P.K. 1979. Children's education in International Children's Year. Bal Bharti. 12 : 39.

Bharti, M. 1990. A comparative study of academic achievement of the 9th class students of public schools and government schools of Chandigarh in relation to intelligence, level of aspiration and achievement motivation. Unpub. M.Sc Thesis, P.U., Chandigarh.

Bhasin, M.P. 1985. The dynamics of teacher-pupil perception. Trends in Education. 12(1) : 16.

Bhaskaran, V. 1989. Women's education key to national development. Social Welfare. 25(2) : 3.

Bisht, G.S. 1972. A study of the level of educational aspiration in relation to socio-economic conditions and educational attainment. Unpub. Ph.D. Thesis, Agra University.

Boehm, R. 1986. Boehm Test of Basic Concepts. The Psychological Corporation, Harcourt Barace Jovonovich, Inc. pp. 1.

Bose, U. 1978. Relationship between parental attitude and academic achievement. Section of Psychology and Educational Science at the 65th Session of Indian Science Congress.

Brown, A., Bransford, J., Ferara, R. and Compione, J. 1983 Learning, remembering and understanding. In J. Flavell and E.M. Markman. Handbook of Child Psychology. Wiley, New York. pp. 61-65.

Braley, R.H., Caldwell, B.M. and Elardo, R. 1977. Family influence on cognitive development. In Hathrington, E.M. and Parke, R.D. Child Psychology—A Contemporary View Point. McGraw-Hill Book Company, New York, pp. 465.

Brim, O.G., Glass, D.C., Neulinger, J. and Firestone, I.J. 1969. American Beliefs and Attitude about Intelligence. Russel Rage Foundation, New York, pp. 60.

Caldwell, B. 1973. Correlates of intellectual performance. In Hathrington. E.M. and Parke, R.D. Child Psychology—A Contemporary View Point. Mc Graw-Hill Book Company, New York. pp. 445.

Camerson, D.M. 1977. Success and failure in the college examination programme and its influence upon occupational and educational aspiration of vocational, technical and adult education teachers. Dissertation Abstracts International. 37(7) : 4064-A.

Cauble, B. 1965. Anxiety in Intermediate Children. Dissertation Abstracts International. 25 : 5150 A.

Charylu, U.N.V. and Reddy, G.N. 1987. Rural women : Decision making, public participation and other basic needs—A study of two villages. Indian Journal of Social Work. 48(4) : 407-475.

Chopra, K. 1970. Out of school activities of high school students. Indian Education Abstract. 16(2) : 10.

Chopra, L. 1969. Effect of certain socio-economic factors on the scholastic achievements of school children. Indian Journal of Psychology. 47(2) : 133-151.

Chopra, S.L. 1964. A study of relationship of socio-economic factors with achievement of the students in the secondary school. Unpub. Ph.D. Thesis, P.U., Chandigarh.

Christian, J.A. 1980. A correlational study of students' performance. Journal of the Institute of Educational Research. 4(1) : 11-25.

Contractor, B.M. 1984. A study of some background factors underlying scholastic performance. Journal of Education and Psychology. 41(4) : 215-219.

Crandall, P., Prestone, A. and Rabsoul, A. 1969. Family influence on cognitive development. In Hathrington, E.M. and Parke, R.D. Child Psychology—A Contemporary View Point, pp. 463.

Crandall, V.J., Dewey, R., Kathovsky, W. and Prestone, A. 1964. Parents' attitudes and behaviour towards children's academic achievements. Journal of Genetic Psychology. 24(1) : 53-56.

Dalela, S.L. 1976. No time to play or dream. Social Welfare. 23(8) : 7.

Daniel, J.C. 1976. Child workers have come to stay. Social Welfare. 23(9) : 5.

Deutsch, M.P. and Brown, B. 1964. Social influences in Negro-White intelligence differences. Journal of Social Issues. 20(2) : 24-35.

Derstine, J.B. 1987. The relationship of anxiety, certain demographic variables and performance in registered nurse students. Dissertation Abstracts International. 48(2) : 309-A.

Deweck. C.S. and Elliot. 1983. Achievement motivation. In Hathrington, E.M. and Parke, R.B. Child Psychology—A Contemporary View Point. Mc Graw-Hill Book Company, New York. pp. 468-473.

Dewey, J. 1916. Democracy and Education. Macmillon Company, New York, pp. 10-11.

Dhami, G.S. 1974. Intelligence, emotional maturity and socio-economic status as factors indicative of success in scholastic achievement. Unpub. Ph.D. Thesis, P.U., Chandigarh.

Dhar, T.N. 1978. Non-formal education. An alternative to universalization of elementary education. Journal of Indian Education. 4(2) : 12.

Elder, G. 1965. Family structure and educational attainment Cross national analysis. American Sociological Review. 30(1) : 81-96.

Feld, S., Ruhlund, D. and Gold, M. 1979. Cognitive development. In Hathrington, E.M. and Parke, R.D. Child Psychology – A Contemporary View Point. Mc Graw-Hill Book Company, New York, pp. 445.450.

Ferguson, L.R. 1970. Family influence on cognitive development. In Hathrington, E.M. and Parke, R.D. Child Psychology – A Contemporary View Point. Mc Graw-Hill Book Company, New York, pp. 465.

Feuerstein, R. 1980. Instrumental Enrichment : An Intervention Program for Cognitive Modifiability. University Park Press, Baltimore.

Ganapathy, M. and Singh, A.K. 1981. A study of relationship of SES, sex and urban-rural background with creative thinking abilities of high school children. Indian Journal of Psychology. 56 : 165-180.

Goblin. S. 1964. Effects of stress on the performance of normally anxious and high anxious subjects under chance and skill conditions. Journal of Abnormal Psychology-83 : 466-472.

Gokulnathan, P.P. 1971. A study of educational achievement related to motivation among higher secondary pupils. Indian Psychological Abstracts. 1 (1) : 59-60.

Good, C.V. 1959. Foundation. Dictionary of Education. Second Edition. University of Cincinnati, pp. 20.

Gupta, S.C. 1976. Wastage and stagnation in elementary school education in India. Education Quarterly. 28 (3) : 35.

Han, Y. 1987. Predictors of educational aspiration and achievement among Asian black, Hispanic and Caucasian adolescents. Dissertation Abstracts. 47 (11) : 4423-A.

Hathrington, E.M. and Parke, R.D. 1986. Child Psychology—A Contemporary View Point. Mc Graw-Hill Book Company, New York. pp. 463-475.

Herold, T. 1971. Social Foundation of Education. John Wiley and Sons, New York, pp. 151-170.

Hill, K.T. 1980. Motivation, evalation and educational testing policy. In Fyans, L.J. Achievement Motivation : Recent Trends in Theory and Research. Plenum, New York. pp. 49-54.

Hussain, M.O. 1977. A study of academic attainment in relation to level of aspiration and anxiety. NCERT, New Delhi.

Indira, R. and Sujatha, B.N. 1988. Equality of educational opportunity for women in India : Myth or reality. Perspectives in Education. 4 (2) : 97-104.

Ismail, R. 1975. Little girl's rights. Yojna. 19 (22) ; 4.

Jackson, B. and Marsden, S.K. 1976. Education and the working class. In Nobbs, J., Robert, H. and Flemning, M.K. Sociology. Macmillan Education Ltd., pp. 85.

Jagannathan, K. 1986. Socio-economic status and academic achievement. Journal of Educational Research and Extension. 22 (3) : 141-149.

Jorapur, S. 1972. Literacy and age at marriage. Social Welfare. 10 (3) : 57-59.

Joseph, M.G. 1973. A study of relationship between the educational environment of the home and student achievement at two different grade levels. Dissertation Abstracts, International 34 (4) : 1178-A.

Kanitkar, T. 1988. Aspiration of decision-makers for the education of girls, Bihar. Indian Journal of Social Work. 49 (2) : 165-167.

Kanta Devi. A study of functioning of Anganwadi centres with regard to child health services. Unpub. Thesis, H.A.U., Hisar.

Kashyap, S.S. 1974. Impact of women's education. Education Quarterly. 21 (2) : 28.

Kaur, A. 1961. An investigation into the degree of correlation between (a) economic status of parents and scholastic achievements of their children; (b) educational status of parents and scholastic achievements of their children. Unpub. M. Ed. Thesis, P.U., Chandigarh.

Kaur, J. 1988. Academic achievement in relation to locus of control, self-concept and achievement motivation at the secondary stage. Unpub. M. Phil. Thesis, P.U., Chandigarh.

Kelly, J.A. and Worell, L. 1977. Family influence on cognitive development. In Hathrington, E.M. and Parke, R.D. Child Psychology—A Contemporary View Point. Mc Graw-Hill Book Company, New York, pp. 465.

Khanna, K.K. 1977. Effectivity of follow up material for girl drop-outs in in a slum of Delhi. Indian Journal of Adult Education. 38 (12) : 10.

Kharangar, Usha, 1983. A study of achievement motivation in boys of selected schools of Hisar city. Unpub, M.Sc. Thesis, H.A.U., Hisar.

Kharb, Deepika. 1990. A study of creativity, language and school achievement of rural and urban children in age group of 10-12 years. Unpub. M.Sc. Thesis, H.A.U., Hisar.

Kingra, J.S. 1986. A study of achievement motivation in relation to socio-economic status and academic achievement. Unpub. M.Ed. Thesis. P.U., Chandigarh.

Kirpal Kaur. 1976. Achievement motivation and anxiety as related to academic success in mathematics. Unpub. M.Ed. Thesis, P.U., Chandigarh.

Kitchen, H.E. 1976. Effect of Parent involvement on the academic success of junior high school students. Dissertation Abstracts International. 36 (11) : 7325-A.

Klaus, R.A. and Gray, S.W. 1968. Cognitive intervention studies. In Hathrington, E. M. and Parke, R.D. Child Psychology—A Contemporary View Point. Mc Graw-Hill Book Company, New York, pp. 473 474.

Kundu, C.L. 1977. Personality Development—A Critique of Indian Studies. Vishal Publishers, New Delhi.

Lakshmi, S.A. 1967. A study on the relationship between the rate of learning and achievement motive among high school boys. Journal of Psychological Research. 11 (1) : 28-31.

Lavin, D.E. 1965. The prediction of academic performance, In Carl, W. and Paul, F.S. A Social-Psychological View of Education. Harcourt. Brace and World Inc.. New York. pp. 8.

Lazar, I. and Darlington, R. 1982. Lasting Effects of Early Education. A report from the consortium of longitudinal studies. Monographs of the Society for Research in Child Development. 47 (2) : 196.

Madho, V. 1977. Levels of aspiration and life goals of Punjab University students in relation to their achievement. Unpub. M.Ed. Thesis, P.U., Chandigarh.

Mantro, D. 1979. A relationship between academic aspiration, success in academic achievement and furture life satisfaction among arts and science undergraduate students. Unpub. M.Ed. Thesis, P.U., Chandigarh.

Mani, S 1980. Causes of drop-outs. Social Welfare. 27 (2) : 17.

Mathur, S.S. and Hundal, B.S, 1972. School achievement and intelligence in relation to some socio-economic background factors. Journal of Educational Psycholoyy. 30 (1) : 42.

McClelland, D.C.. Atkinson, J.W., Clark, R.A. and Lowell, E.L. 1955. The Achievement Motive. Appleton-Century-Crafts, New York. pp. 70-76.

Medsker, L.L. 1963. Factors related to college attendance and performance in high school graduates. In Cole, S.B. Social Foundation of Education ; Environmental Influences in Teaching and Learning, John Wiley and Sons, Inc. New York. pp. 51-53.

Mehar, R. 1991. A study of achievement motivation in relation to socio-economic status and academic achievement of high school students of rural and urban areas of Karnal district. Unpub. M.Ed. Thesis, P.U., Chandigarh.

Mehra, S. 1977. Education of women in rural Haryana. Kurukshetra 25 (15) : 35.

Mehta, p. 1966. Level of 'n' achievement in high school boys. Indian Educational Review. 2 (2) : 165.

Mehta, P. 1964. Achievement motive in high school boys. Indian Psychological Abstracts. 7 (2) : 139-140.

Mehta, P.K. 1977. Fducation in rural India. Kurukshetra. 26 (19) : 5.

Miller, J. 1967, Cognitive intervention studies. In Hathrington, E.M. and Parke, R.D. Child Psychology—A Contemporary View Point. Mc Graw Hill Book Company, pp. 473.

Mittal, R. and Nand, H. 1984. Why they drop out ? Social Welfare. 3 (7) : 34-35.

Mohanty, G. 1972. Level of aspiration as a function of sex, socio-economic factors and class performance. Unpub. Ph. D. Thesis. Utkal University, NCERT, New Delhi.

Muralidharan, R. 1980. Compensatory education for disadvantage children. Social Welfare. 23 (4) : 12.

Muthayya, B.C, 1962. Level of aspiration and intelligence of high achievers and low achievers in the scholastic field. Journal of Psychological Researches. 6 (1) : 15.

Nair, A.S, 1980. Effect of general and test anxiety on cognitive performance in mathematics. Quest in Education. 17 (3) : 19.

Nobbs, J., Robert, H. and Flemming, M.E. 1976. Sociology. Macmillan Education Ltd. pp. 89.

Ojha, P,G.K. 1966. Important factors in the development of compulsory education. In progress of Compulsory Education, Universal Publications, New Delhi. pp. 319.

Pal, R.P., Jain, S. and Tiwari, G. 1985. Self concept and level of aspiration in high and low achieving higher secondary pupils. Perspectives in Psychological Researches. 8 (2) : 49-53.

Pandey, K. and Solanki, H. 1975. An experiment try out of the effect of increased level of aspiration on achievement. Journal of Psychological Research 3 : 10-13.

Parikh. P.A. 1978. A study of achievement motivation, school performance and educational norms of secondary school pupils of standards VIII, IX and X in the city of Bombay. Indian Education Review. 13 (3) : 57-63.

Parsons, J.E. 1982. Expectancies, values and academic behaviours. In Spence, J.T. Perspectives on Achievement and Achievement Motivation. Mc Graw-Hill Book Company, New York.

Parsons, J.E.. Adler, T.J. and Kaczola, C.M. 1982. Cognitiue Development. In Hathrington, E.M. and Parke, R.D. child Psychology—A Contemporary Vivew Point. Mc Graw-Hill Book Company, pp. 462.

Pillai, N. 1975. Educational progress and success in rural areas. Indian Dissertation Abstracts. 4 (3) :102.

Plowden's Report. 1967. Central Advisory council for Education. Children and their Primary Schools, H.M.S.O., London.

Ports, A. and Wilson, K.C. 1976. Black-white differences in educational attainment. American Sociological Review 41 (6) : 414-431.

Pressey Robusen and Herroch. 1941. Academic or scholastic. Achievement. In Rao, S.N. Educational Psychology. Wiley Eastern Limited, New Delhi. pp. 293.

Puri, N. 1991. The Child Survival. Population Education News, pp. 4-7.

Radin, N. 1976. The role of the father in cognitive, academic and intellectual development. In Lamb, M.E. The Role of Father in Child Development. Wiley Interscience, New York. pp. 71-72.

Rai, S. 1971. Education an important aspect of development. Education Quarterly 23 (1): 10.

Rai. S. 1975. Education of our rural folk. Education Quarterly. 27 (2): 18.

Rajguru, G., Satpathy and Dass. P.C. 1975. Academic achievement of students-Impact of parents and socio-religion factors. Education Quarterly. 26 (4): 41.

Rajput, A.S. 1984. Study of academic achievement of students mathematics in relation to their intelligence, achievement motivation and socio-economic status. Unpub. Ph. D. Thesis, P.U., Chandigarh.

Ramey, C.T., Bryant, D., Sparking, J.T. and Wasik, B.H. 1985. Educational interventions to enhance intellectual development. In Harel, S. and Nastasion, N. The At-risk Infant; Psycho, Socio, Medico Aspects, Paul, H Books, Baltimore pp. 75-79.

Rao, Y.R. 1976. A study of the relationships of few selected variables to the academic achievement indices of secondary schools. Indian Dissertation Abstracts. 5 (4): 203.

Raynor, C. 1970. Effect of achievement motivation and future orientation level of performance. Journal of Personality and Social Psychology. 17 (1): 36-41.

Reed, E.W. and Reed, R.C. 1965. Family influence on cognitive development. In Hathrington, E.M. and Parke, R.D. Child Psychology – A Contemporary View Point. Mc Graw-Hill Book Company, New York, pp. 466.

Rosen, B.C. and D'Andrade, R.C. 1959. The psychological origin of achievement motivation. In Miller, H.L. and Woock, R.R. Social Foundation of Urban Education. Halt, Hinecart and Winston, Inc., pp 195.

Routray, D.K. 1988. Effect of self concept, school attendence, teachers' involvement and attitude on the academic achievement of gifted, average and failed students. Unpub- M. Phil. Thesis, P.U., Chandigarh.

Ruble, D.N., Boggiono, A.K., Feldman, N.S. and Loeblo, J.H. 1980. Developmental Psychology. Mc Graw-Hill Book company, New York.

Saleh, S. 1985. A study of the influence of schooling, student background and academic ability on student academic achievement in Indonesian's Public General Senior High Schools. Dissertation Abstracts International. 46 (4): 946-A.

Saini, B.K. 1977. Academic achievement as a function of economic status and educational standard of parents. Psychological Studies. 22 (2): 24-27.

Sarason, S.B. and Mandler, G. 1952. Some correlates of test anxiety. Journal of Abnormal Social Psychology. 47: 810-17.

Saraswathi, J.S. and Gupta, Radhika. 1985, Educate a woman and you educate a family. Perspective in Education. 1 (1): 49-54.

Saroj Bala, 1980. Socio-economic factors affecting the scholastic achievements of the children in rural Haryana. Unpub. M.Sc. Thesis, H.A.U., Hisar.

Sen Gupta, p. 1976. Child labour as a social problem. Social Welfare. 22 (11): 1.

Shah, N. 1991. Education A chance. The Sunday Tribune, September 22.

Shah, S. and Nagia, M. 1984. The crusade for literacy. Review of Educational Research. 26 (1): 132.

Sharma, M.K. 1982. Academic achievement of school students vis-a-vis their parents' education. Asian Journal of Psychology and Education. 9 (2): 22-28.

Shamsuddin, S. 1975. Educational progress. Review of Educational Research. 45 (2): 450.

Shankar, U. and Kundu, C.L. 1970: Education in Haryana: Retrospect and Prospect. Published by Department of Education, Kurukshetra University, Kurukshetra.

Shulka, K.L. 1983. Factors differentiating high and low academic performance of secondary schools in Rajasthan. University of Udaipur. Indian Dissertation Abstracts. 16 (2): 14.

Siddique, A.G., Tewari, G.S. and Sultana, M. 1983. Factors affecting academic achievement of school children. Journal of Educational Psychology. 41 (3): 126-132.

Singh, A. 1962. Socio-economic background of students and their performance in examinations. Unpub. M.A. Thesis, P.U., Chandigarh.

Singh, B. 1969. Students problems with regard to fathers' occupation. South Indian Teacher. 41 (8): 235-238.

Singh, B. 1988. Promoting pre-school age education. Education Quarterly. 40 (3): 26-29.

Singh, K. 1974. Scholastic achievements of high school students in relation to intelligence, anxiety and adjustment Unpub. M. Ed. Thesis, P.U., Chandigarh.

Singh, L. 1991. A study of achievement motivation in relation to home environment and academic achievement. Unpub. M. Ed, Thesis, P.U., Chandigarh.

Singh, M.C.P. 1973. Impact of father's occupation and social status upon scholastic achievements. Indian Psychological Abstracts. 4 (2) 90.

Sinha, M. 1973. Educational achievement. Review of Educational Research. 25 (2): 15.

Skiera, E. 1980. The progressive education movement and schools in Europe: Development, teaching method profiles, perspective Education. 41: 7-28.

Smith, L.P.1966. The influence of testing conditions on need for achievement scores and their relationship to performance scores. In Atkinson, J.W. and Feather, N.T. A theory of Achievement Motivation. John Wiley and Sons, New York, pp. 277-297.

Soman, K. 1977. Some effective correlates of mathematics' achievement of secondary school students. Unpub. Ph.D.

Thesis, University of Kerala.

Srivastava, S.S. and Singh, D.R. 1975. SES and achievement motivation among teacher trainees. Journal of Education and Psychology. 33 (3): 129-135.

Stephans, J.H. 1958. Educational Psychology. Hamery Holt and Company, New York, pp. 220.

Sudha, B.G. and Tiwari, S. 1985. Child labour in rural areas-some factors. Kurukshetra. 3: 31-36.

Sween. 1984. Academic achievement of high school students in relation to the instructional design intelligence, self-concept and n-achievement. Unpub. Ph.D. Thesis, P.U., Channigarh.

Talesra, H.L. 1986. Higher education among women: A analysis of the situation in a district of India. Perspectives in Education. 2 (2): 121-124.

Tandani, B. 1984. Investigating relationship between achievement motivation and academic achievement of socially deprived students. Journal of Education. 20(3): 13-16.

Trow, A.C. 1956. Psychology in Teaching. Houghton Mittilian Company, Baston. pp. 16.

Ulldriks, G. Social disadvantage and educational opportunity. In Eggleston, M. Contemporary Research in the Sociology of Education. Mathuen and Co. Ltd., pp. 23.

Venkata Subramanian, R. and Kulandaivel, K. 1968. A study of causes of absenteeism of some secondary school pupil in Coimbatore. Journal of Education, Research and Extension, 4 (4): 145-153.

Vora, I.A. 1977. A study of reading comprehension in the context of attitude, anxiety and 'n' achievement. Journal of Education and Psychology. 35(1): 46-57.

White, D.W. 1987. Relationship between school climate and classroom climate between school climate and student achievement and between classroom climate and student achievement. Dissertation Abstracts International. 48 (2): 282-A.

Willerman, E.L and Stanfford R.E. 1972. Behaviour Genetics. John Wiley and Sons, New York. pp. 321-325.

Zajone, R.B. 1976. Family configuration and intelligence. Science, pp. 227-236.

Index

Abrahasan, 11
Aggarwal, 17
Ahluwalia, 13
Ahuja, 23
Annamalai, 27
Aristotle, 1
Atkinson, 26

Bartlette, 26
Bhandari, 23, 64, 97, 120
Bhangod, 24
Bhargawa, 18, 38, 39, 72
Bharti, 28
Bhasin, 136
Bhaskaran, 18, 62, 64, 97, 120
Bishit, 27
Beehm, 144
Bose, 19, 119
Bradley, 130
Brim, 27
Brown, 138

Caldwell, 142
Cameron, 27, 119
Cauble, 26
Charyulu, 20
Chopra, 11, 12, 16, 117
Christian, 25, 30
Contractor, 14, 62, 106, 119
Crandall, 19, 138

Dalela, 17
D' Andrede, 16, 138
Daniels, 21, 86, 120
Darlington, 142
Deepika, 117
Derstine, 27
Desai, Morarji, 5
Deutsch, 11
Deweek, 138
Dewey, 1
Dhami, 13, 117
Dhar, 17

Education status of Women, 19, 146
- Academic achievements of, 7
- Barriers in education of girls, 89
- Defination of, 1
- Girls education in Haryana, 4
- In 19th century, 3
- In society, 2-3
- Intellectual level of mother, 5-6
- Limitation of study, 9
- Objectives of, 9, 146-47
- Origin of 1
- Proper schooling of girls, 6-7, 146
- Scholastic achievement, 7
- Scope of study, 9
- Spread after independence, 4-8
- Spread in Haryana, 3-4
- Stress on, 2
- Suggested areas for further research, 151

Elder, 12
Elliot, 138

Feld, 137
Ferguson, 130
Feuerstein, 139
Fraser, 3

Gandhi, Mahatma, 5
Ganpathy, 13
Gareth, 43
Goblin, 119
Gokulnathan, 24
Good, 7
Gorbin, 26
Gray, 142
Gupta, 21, 35, 38, 39, 71, 86, 120

Han, 28
Harthrington, 131
Herold, 4
Herroch, 7
Hill, 130
Hundal, 13, 106, 112
Hussain, 27

Indira, 4
Ismail, 16, 62, 86, 120

Jackson, 17
Jagannath, 15
Jorapur, 22
Joseph, 16, 120

Kanitkar, 28
Kanta, 143
Kashyap, 23
Kaur, 11, 26
Kelly, 130
Khanna, 17, 62
Kharangar, Usha, 25
Kharb, 15
Kirgra, 25
Kirpal Kaur, 24, 26, 119
Kitchen, 21
Klaus, 142
Kulandaivel, 16
Kulshreshtha, 34, 38
Kundu, 3, 13, 117
Lakshmi, 24

Lazar, 142
Litwin, 26

Madho, 28, 119
Madler, 26
Mani, 14, 64, 112
Mantro, 28
Marsden, 17
Maslow, 7
Mc Clelland, 137
Medskar, 11, 106, 116
Mehar, 26
Mehra, 19, 119
Mehta, 12, 19, 24, 117
Methodology, 29-43
  Attitude towards girls education, 36
  Constraints in girl education, 37
  Data analysis, 42-43
    chi-square test, 43
    Critical ratio, 42-43
    Percentnge, 42
    Rank correlation, 43
    Rediability coefficients, 42
  Data collection, 41-42
  Economic variables, 34-35
    Annual income, 34-35
    Land owned, 34
    Occupation, 34
  Education, 32
  Locale of research, 29
  Ordinal position, 32
  Psychological variables, 35-36
    Academic anxiety, 35
    Achievement motivation, 35
    Attainment discrepancy score, 36
    Goal discrepancy score, 36
    Level of aspiration, 35-36
    Number of times goal reach store, 36
  Sampling procedure, 29-30
    Section of district, 29
    Selection of respondents, 30
    Selection of villages, 29-30

Social variables. 32-36
Caste, 33
Family structure, 33
Number of children, 33
Size of family, 32
Social participation, 33-34
Socio economic status, 34
Type of family, 32
Tools used for data collection, 37-41
Academic anxiety scale for children, 39
Attitude towards girl education, 39-40
Item analysis, 40
Item collection, 39-40
Constraint questionnaire, 40-41
Level of aspiration scale, 39
Rao's achievement motivation test, 37-38
Reliability of scale, 40
Validity of scale, 39, 40
Variables and measurement, 30-32
Dependent variable, 30-31
Independent variable, 31
Personal variable, 31-32

Michel, 43
Miller, 142
Mittal, 15
Mohanty, 27
Muralidharan, 18, 62, 120
Muthayya, 27, 119

Nagia, 19, 119
Nair, 119
Nand, 15
Narasimha Rao, P.V., 2

Ojha, 16, 64, 97
Pal, 28
Pandey, 27
Parikh, 25, 117
Parka, 131
Parsons, 129, 139
Pillai, 23, 63, 120
Plowden, 12
Plowden, 106, 117
Ports, 14
Punjab Primary Act 1919, 4
Puri, 5

Radhika, 20, 21, 86, 96, 119, 125
Radin, 130
Rai, 19, 20, 85, 125
Rajguru, 131, 106
Rajput, 25
Ramey, 142
Roas Achievement Motivation Test, 25, 35, 37-38, 71, 140
Raynor, 26
Reed, 5
Results and discussion, 44-145
Home constraints, 73-89
Community constraints, 83-86, 149
Community disapproval of girl sitting and studing while parents at work, 83-84
Early marriage of girl, 85
Insecurity for girls, 84
Lack of community support, 84
Less number of girls attending school, 84
More importance to home and field work, 84
Other girls of community involved in household work, 84
Contract scores, 87-89
Community constraints, 87-89
Composite constraint score, 89
Home constraint, 87
Personal constraints, 87
School constraints, 73-77,

149
Home constraints, 73-77, 149
Family conflict, 77
Lack of family assistance in teaching and grouping, 77
Lack of proper light facility at home, 77
Lack of separate study place, 77
Lack of time, 76-77
Large family size, 73
Prolonged illness of family members, 77
Personal constraints, 82-83, 149
Early marriage and parent-in-laws, negative attitude towards education, 83
Health problems of student, 83
Internal inhibition while asking questions in class-room, 83
Lack of interest in studies, 82
Lack of job opportunities, 83
Lack of parental support and encouragement, 83
Unfair examination system, 83
School constraints, 78-82, 149
Curriculum problems, 80-81
Difficulty improper grasp of subject matter, 80-81
Heavy Work load, 81
Lack of pre-hand preparations, 81
More time spent on games, 81
Non-interesting presentation of material in books, 81
Over-crowding in each class, 81
Teaching methoods, 81
Expensive trading, 78
Non-availabiity of books, 79
At shops, 79
In library, 79
To purchase, 79
Other school problems, 81-82, 149
Corporal punishment, 81-82
Faulity examination system, 82
Indiscipline caused by boys, 82
Indulgence in quarels, 82
Long distance between residence and school, 82
Non-conducive school environment, 82
Poor physical facilities, 78
Lack of drinking water facility, 78
Lack of library facility, 78
Lack of toilet facility, 78
Poor classroom physical facilities, 78
Staff facility, 79-80
Conflict among teachers, 80
Duty delegation to students, 80
Lack of lady teachers, 79
Lack of teachers, 79
Lack of teachers interest, 79
Teachers getting personel work done by students, 80
Teachers rude behaviour, 79
Teachers stress on private tention, 80

Unfair judgement by teachers, 80
Perceived constraints and attitude, 51-73, 148
Community constraints, 60-65, 148-49
Community preference to activities other than education, 61
Early marriage of girls, 61
Feeling of guilt while not assisting parents in work, 60
Lack of community support in creating conducive environment, 60
More-importance given to home/field work, 61
Prevailing insecurity, 61
Uncommon practice in village, 61
Constraints perceived by girl respondents, 73
Constraints scores, 65-68
Community constraints, 66-67
Composite constraint scores, 68
Home constraints, 65-66
Personal constraints, 66
Economic variables, 55
Annual income, 55, 148
Land owned, 55
Socio-economic status, 55
Family background of girl respondents, 51, 148
Frequency distribution of girl respondents, 73
Home constraints, 56-59, 148
Illness of family members, 59
Lack of family assistance in teaching and guides, 56
Lack of interest in educating girls, 59
Lack of light facility at home, 59
Lack of time, 56
Large family size, 56
Low family income, 56
Information about girl respondents, 69
Ordinal position of girls, 69
Parents attitude towards girls education, 68-69
Performance on psychological tests, 70-72
Academic anxiety, 70, 149
Achievement motivation, 70
Aspiration level, 71
Attainment discrepency score, 71
Number of times goal reach score, 72
Personal constraints, 59-60, 148
Health problems of students, 59-60
In laws displeasure on continuing education, 60
Lack of faith in fairness in examination, 60
Lack of girls interest, 59
Limited job opportunities, 60
Personal variables, 51-54
Fathers age, 51
Fathers education, 53
Mothers education, 53
Psychological variables of parents, 55-59
Social variables, 54-58
Caste, 54
Family size, 54
Family structure, 54
Family type, 54
Number of children, 54
Social participation, 54-55
Scholastic achievements, 44-51, 147-48

Average marks obtained in eight and ninth classes, 44-47, 147
Drop-out rate, 49-50, 148
Failing percentage, 50-51
Perceived caused of drop-out, 50
Performance of respondents subject-wise, 47-49, 147-48
Scholastic achievement of girl students, 98-125, 150
Association between economic variables and, 113-17
Annual income and, 114-15
Land owned, 115-17
Occupation of failure, 114
Association between family background variables and, 95
Association between personal variables and, 99-104
Parental age, 99-101
Parental education, 101-04
Association between social variables and, 106-13
Caste, 110-11
Family size, 107-08
Family structure, 109-10
Family type, 106-07
Number of children in family, 108-09
Social participation, 111-13
Association between socio economic status and, 117-20
Multiple regression analysis of independent variables, 120-22
Teachers attitude and perceived constraints, 122-25
Coostraints perceived by teachers, 123-25
Teachers attitude, 122-23
Strategy for enhancing scholastic achievements of girls students, 125-45, 150-51
Home related problems, 126-35
Home constraints, 131-35
Parental attitude, 128-31
Parental illetracy, 126-28
School related constraints, 135-44
Curriculum problems, 139-40
Early stimulation, 140-44
Students problems, 136-39
Teachers problems, 135-36
Social constraints, 144-45
Teachers viewpoint, 90-98, 149
Constraint scores, 97-98, 150
Constraints perceived by, 93-97
Comprehension of subject-matter, 93
Discipline problems in coeducational schools, 95
Household chores, 96
Interest in studies, 93
Male teachers behaviour, 96
Poor enrolement of girls, 96
Punctuality, 95
Punishment problem, 96
Regularity in home works, 93-95
School attendence, 95
Shyness and hesitation, 95
General information about teachers, 90
Teachers attitude towards girls education, 90-93
Review of literature, 1-8, 10-28
Famillial factors and scholastic achievements, 10-20
Attitude and values of parents, 19-20
Family background, 10-15
Home constraints, 15-19
Psychological characteristics, 24-26
Academic anxiety, 26-27
Achievement motivation, 24-26

Level of aspiration, 27-28
School and community related factors, 20-24
Community related factors, 22-24
School factors, 20-22

Robysen, Pressey, 7
Rosen, 16, 138
Routray. 22, 123
Ruble, 139
Saini, 13
Salah, 21, 120
Sarason, 26
Saraswathi, 20, 21, 86, 96, 119, 125
Saroj Bala, 18, 47, 62
Sen Gupta, 17
Shah, 19, 22, 39, 85, 119, 120
Shamsuddin, 23
Shankar, 3
Sharma, 14, 106
Shukla, 21, 85, 128
Shyam, 13
Siddique, 14, 117
Singh, 11, 12, 13, 20, 26, 35, 38, 39, 71, 72, 86, 116, 117, 119
Sinha, 3, 19, 116, 119
Skiera, 22, 62, 86, 120
Smith, 26
Solanki, 27
Soman, 26, 119
Spearman, 43
Srivastava, 13, 117
Stanfort, 131
Stephans, 11
Sudha, 18, 62
Sujatha, 4
Swen, 28
Talesra, 23, 63, 120

Thomson, James, 3
Tiwari, 18, 62
Trivedi, 33
Trow, 7
Uldriks, 19
Venkata Subramanian, 16, 27
Vora, 25
White, 22
Willerman, 131
Worell, 130
Zajone, 14, 112